The Oral Law

מגיד

MAGGID

Chaim H. Schimmel

The Oral Law

The Rabbinic Contribution to *Torah sheBe'al Peh*

with notes & comments by
HaGaon HaRav Simcha Wasserman *zt"l*

Maggid Books

The Oral Law
The Rabbinic Contribution to Torah sheBe'al Peh

First Maggid Edition, 2019

Maggid Books
An imprint of Koren Publishers Jerusalem Ltd.

POB 8531, New Milford, CT 06776-8531, USA
& POB 4044, Jerusalem 9104001, Israel
www.maggidbooks.com

ISBN 978-1-59264-534-3, *hardcover*

A CIP catalogue record for this title is available from the British Library

Printed and bound in the United States

RABBI MOSES FEINSTEIN
455 F. D. R. DRIVE
New York, N. Y. 10002
—
ORegon 7-1222

משה פיינשטיין
ר"מ תפארת ירושלים
בנוא יארק

בע"ה

הנה בא לפני מהר"ר חיים שיפמעל שליט"א מלאנדרן והראה לי ספרו "התורה שבעל פה" ובקש הסכמתי עליו. ובאחר שנכתב בשפת אנגלית, מסרתיו לנכדי, הרה"ג מוהר"ר מרדכי טנדלר שליט"א שקראו לגמרי ושבחו מאד לפני, כספר שמבאר באופן מבורר וקל להבין, בראיות ומקורות, כמה יסודות עיקריות בענין התורה שבעל פה.

ועל כן הרינו שולח בזה ברכתי להמחבר שליט"א, שיצליחהו השי"ת בהפרצת ספרו זה, ושיהיה לתועלת להרבות בכלל ישראל ידיעת היסודות אודות תורתינו הקדושה, ושיגרום הרבצת תורה שבזכותה נזכה כולנו בקרוב להרמת קרן התורה ע"י משיח צדקינו.

הכו"ח לכבוד התורה ביום כ"א שבת תשמ"ג בנוא יארק.

משה פיינשטיין

משה פיינשטיין

heichal hatorah betzion
היכל התורה בציון
ראש הישיבה הרב צבי קושלבסקי Rosh Yeshiva: Rabbi Zvi Kushelevsky
ע"ר 580047009

בס"ד

כ"א אדר פרשת ויקהל פקודי תשס"ו

הובא לפני הספר "THE ORAL LAW" מאת ידידי הרב חיים שימל שליט"א, עברתי על חלק ניכר מן הספר, כולל התוספות שבמהדורה החדשה, ומצאתי אותו כולו מחמדים מיוסד על דברי הראשונים וגדולי האחרונים, שבו הוא מבאר את יסודות תורה שבעל פה, ומגלה מקורות מעיינות החכמה, ומראה את הזיקה של חכמינו ז"ל אל נותן התורה.

ניכר שהמחבר עמל רבות כדי שיצא מתחת ידו דברים ברורים הכתובים בבהירות רבה ובסגנון אשר יאפשר לקורא להבין גם את הדברים הקשים ביותר קלות.

אם כי הספר נועד בתחילתו לקהל הרחב, אבל בטוחני שגם בני ישיבה יוכלו להפיק תועלת מהקריאה בו.

ואין לי אלא לברכו, יהא רעוא מן שמיא, שדבריו יתקבלו בבי מדרשא ויפוצו מעינותיו חוצה להגדיל תורה ולהאדירה, אמן.

החותם לכבוד התורה ולומדיה,

צבי קושלבסקי

רחוב קצנלבוגן 92, ת.ד. 43106, ירושלים 91430 . 92 Katzenelbogen St. P.O.B 43106 Jerusalem 91430, Israel
טלפון: 6519402 פקס: 6524402 Tel: 6519402 Fax: 6524402

To the memory of my parents ז"ל

Contents

Foreword xi

Acknowledgments xvii

Introduction xix

Chapter 1: The Origin of the Oral Law 1

Chapter 2: Laws Derived by Rabbinic Interpretation 27

Chapter 3: Halachah and Morality – the Moral Svara 49

Chapter 4: Laws Created by Rabbinic Legislation 59

Chapter 5: Torah min haShamayim and Rabbinic Interpretation and Legislation 81

Chapter 6: Restrictions on Rabbinic Legislation 93

Chapter 7: Legal Fictions, the Spirit of the Law, and Lifnim Mishurat haDin 113

Chapter 8: The Mishnah of the Sages 135

Afterword: The Talmud and the Talmid 159

Index of Sources and Authorities 163

Foreword

I have loved the Torah of R. Chaim (Harry) Schimmel ever since I first encountered it and him. He brings a penetrating mind and a loving heart to "the word of God; that is, Jewish law." His Torah always strives to be *emet le'amito* – not just about truth on the surface but also its connection to a deeper truth beneath. That is the difference – and it is all the difference – between being clever and being wise. The insights of this book are wise.

One of the striking features of *The Oral Law* is its insistence on getting to fundamentals, in particular the tension between two essential truths: first, that there is nothing within the Oral Law that was not already given to Moshe at Sinai; second, acknowledgement of the remarkable contributions made by our Sages themselves, that made them conclude that in some sense "a Sage is greater than a prophet." They knew how to hear the voice of Sinai and distill it into rules of action, so that God's will could become real in the life of the community, the Divine word translated into human deed.

One of the particular fascinations of this new edition is its important chapter on the moral *svara*, the rabbinic axiom that the morality of the Torah is fundamental to its interpretation. That fact cannot be sufficiently emphasized. The Sages knew that this was at the heart of the Judaic enterprise. In the only place in the Torah that explains why God chose Avraham, we read: "For I have chosen him so that he will instruct his children and his household after him that they may keep the way of the Lord by doing what is right and just…" (*Bereshit* 18:19). Doing right and justice stand at the core of the Torah's enterprise.

Interestingly, the prophet Hoshea added two other key words: "I will betroth you to me forever; I will betroth you in right and justice, loving-kindness and compassion" (2:19). Why the difference? Because Avraham, as the first Jew, lived in a world of strangers, and in such a world the operative principles are the relatively thin ones of right and justice. That is an ethic between strangers. Hoshea belongs to a time many centuries later when Jews had long been a people in their own land, and as not just a nation but an extended family, they were bound not only by thin imperatives of right and justice but also by the thick bonds of loving-kindness and compassion.

When we speak of the moral *svara*, it is important to note that the Sages traced their ancestry not to the priests but the prophets: "Moshe received the Torah at Sinai and handed it to Yehoshua, Yehoshua to the elders, the elders to the prophets, and the prophets handed it to the men of the Great Assembly" (*Avot* 1:1). It was the prophets who – more eloquently than anyone else in history – were the moral voice of the nation, telling it time and again that it was not simply military strength, however important that was, but moral and spiritual strength that would ultimately decide its fate. The Sages saw themselves as their heirs.

How are we to understand the connection between bold ethical principles of the Torah and the prophets and the detailed exposition of Jewish law that we associate with the Sages? There are two key texts here. One is Ramban's commentary on the verse: "You shall do the right and the good" (*Devarim* 6:18):

> Our rabbis have a fine interpretation of this. They said, "This refers to compromise and going beyond the requirement of the law." The intent of this is that initially he [Moshe] had said that you shall observe the laws and the statutes which He has commanded you. Now he says that with respect to what He has not commanded, you should likewise take heed to do what is good and the right in His eyes, for He loves the good and the right. And

> this is a great matter, for it is impossible to mention in the Torah all a person's actions towards his neighbors and acquaintances, or his commercial activity, or all his social and political institutions. So after He had mentioned many of them, such as: "You shall not go about as a tale bearer," "You shall not take vengeance or bear a grudge," "You shall not curse the deaf," "You shall rise up before the elderly," and the like, He continues to say generally that one should do the good and the right in all matters, including compromise and going beyond the strict letter of the law ...[1]

The Torah gives many examples of ethical imperatives. But one cannot spell out the whole of the ethical life, much of which is too situational and time-bound to lend itself to an exhaustive set of principles. Hence the Torah adds in general terms: "You shall do the right and the good," indicating that there is an entire area where the Torah expects moral behavior from us, even though this involves going beyond what it explicitly commands.

Further clarification comes from the second source, Rabbi Vidal of Tolosa, in his work *Maggid Mishneh*:

> Our perfect Torah sets forth general principles for the cultivation of virtue and good behavior. The statement "you shall be holy" means, as the rabbis said: "Sanctify yourself in what is permitted to you," so that you should not be overindulgent in the satisfaction of your desires. Similarly, the Torah says: "You shall do the right and good," meaning that you should deal well and uprightly with people. It was not appropriate in all this to command details, because the commandments of the Torah are obligatory for every period, all time and in every circumstance, but the virtues of human beings and their conduct vary according to the time and the people concerned. The Sages of blessed memory specified some useful particulars included under these principles, some of which they made binding law, others recommendations before

1. Ramban on *Devarim* 6:18.

> the fact but not binding or actionable after the fact, and still other rules for those who seek the way of special piety.[2]

The *Maggid Mishneh* is telling us that the Sages, knowing that the Torah's ethical concerns were not restricted to matters explicitly commanded or forbidden, availed themselves of a range of imperatives – some categorical, others aspirational, but in each case carrying through the moral program of the Torah itself. The Sages did not see themselves as moral innovators; to the contrary: if it had not been said at Sinai they could not have taught what they taught. But they recognized that it was their task to bring the sacred word of God down from heaven to earth so that it became real in the lives of the nation as a whole.

The very way that the Torah structures these commandments, by sketching them out in broad strokes rather than comprehensive detail, was itself a mandate to the Sages both to institute certain *Takkanot* and to use the ethical principles of the Torah itself to interpret Halachah.

One of the most interesting elements in the new chapter of the book on the moral *svara* is the distinction between cases where the law itself has a moral dimension, as in the case of the prohibition against putting a stumbling block before the blind, and a case where we say: *ein lecha bo ela chiddusho bilvad,* one cannot extend a stated *chiddush*. R. Schimmel brings the view of R. Shmuel Landau, son of the *Noda B'yehuda,* that a *chiddush* is a command that runs contrary to *svara*. When there is a moral dimension the Sages tended to give an expansive interpretation to the command, but when there was dissonance they gave it a restrictive reading. Moral concern, in other words, was fundamental to the way the Sages interpreted the biblical text, and it determined whether they read it broadly or narrowly. In so doing, they were honoring their self-definition as heirs to the prophets.

The same spirit animates the Sages' *Takkanot*. Think of such principles as *mipnei takkanat hashavim,* certain leniencies in restoring stolen property so as not to make it too difficult for offenders to atone and make restitution. This echoes the spirit of Yechezkel's message: "As surely as

2. *Maggid Mishne* on *Hilchot Shechenim* 14:3.

I live, declares the Sovereign Lord, I take no pleasure in the death of the wicked, but rather that they turn from their ways and live" (33:11).

Or consider the principle *kedei shelo levayesh et mi she'ein lo,* to avoid embarrassing those who are disadvantaged or in need. On certain days of the year when young ladies went out to dance before potential suitors, they wore borrowed clothes so as not to put those who did not have new clothes to shame. The equal dignity of all is implicit in the first chapter of the Torah, which tells us we are all equally in God's image. It would be hard to imagine another society so sensitive to the feelings of the poor.

Or the principle *chasa haTorah al mamonam shel Yisrael,* that the Torah is considerate of the financial concerns of Israel. This was derived from one of the biblical laws of sacrifices and became a general principle of the Sages in cases where they feared that the cost of living a Jewish life was in danger of becoming prohibitive. The poor must have the same access to the Divine as the rich.

One of the most interesting and far-reaching of rabbinic *Takkanot* was the principle of *marit ayin,* the appearance of wrongdoing. There is a difference between this and the principle of *chashad,* suspicion. The latter referred to cases where one is doing something permitted but an observer might think one is doing something forbidden. In such a case we are bound to avoid suspicion under the principle: "You shall be innocent before the Lord and before Israel" (*Bemidbar* 32:22). *Marit ayin* is different. It occurs when people seeing what a person is doing might come to do something forbidden because they do not realize the special circumstances that apply in that person's case. What this implies is remarkable: *We are expected to behave as if we were a living Shulchan Aruch.* Just as a code of law should be unambiguous, so should our conduct be. People should be able to see how we act and from that learn how to live.

These are all profound indications of how interfused morality and Halachah were for the Sages, and how deeply they had internalized the spirit of the prophets from whom they traced their descent, as well as the overarching themes of the Torah itself.

The Oral Law is a fine book by an exceptional Torah scholar. How beautiful it is that this new edition will be published as R. Chaim and his *ezer kenegdo* Hannah have now moved to the Holy City, Jerusalem, where they are both participating in and contributing to the realization of Isaiah's prophecy: "For the Torah shall come forth from Zion" (2:3).

May the book find many new readers and re-readers. They will be enlightened, impressed, and blessed.

בברכה וכבוד רב,

Rabbi Jonathan Sacks

May 2019

Acknowledgments

Vigilance dictates that one should not be excessively vigilant.

(Rabbenu Bachaya Ibn Pekudei,
Introduction to Chovot HaLevavot)

Vigilance would have advised that I do not undertake this work at all. It requires a man very much more qualified than I, to do justice to a subject of such sanctity and magnitude – to analyze the structure of the Oral Law, upon which the entire edifice of traditional Judaism rests.

But I undertook this work because it was of great interest to me, and my lifetime friend, Professor Cyril Domb F.R.S., encouraged R. Yaakov Feldheim to publish my work. I am deeply grateful to my friends for their involvement. The relative success of this book goes to show how wise are the words of Rabbenu Bachaya.

I must now express my thanks to Mr. Matthew Miller and R. Reuven Ziegler, who suggested to me that they would like to publish a new edition of *The Oral Law* at Maggid Books, for their help throughout bringing this volume to fruition.

This gave me the opportunity to add a new chapter and an afterword on Halachah and morality. Above all, it prompted Rabbi Lord Jonathan Sacks to write an erudite and elegant foreword to this new edition. Rabbi Sacks is not only a Torah scholar but also one of the leading Jewish thinkers of our time. Rabbi Sacks and Rabbanit Elaine are generous, warm, and dear friends of our entire family.

There are not many books that have the privilege of a contribution from both HaGaon R. Simcha Wasserman, and להבחל״ח Rabbi Jonathan Sacks.

I remember with gratitude HaRav Shlomo Zalman Auerbach, who always made me welcome in his home and gave me generously of his time. I had the privilege to raise with him, on occasions, some of the issues discussed in this book. In his presence, one had the unique "vision of greatness" to which I refer in the Introduction.

I must also express my thanks to R. Ephraim Landau, who edited R. Simcha's hand-written notes, and to my dear nephew Mark Schonfeld, who kept me on the right side of copyright law.

Finally, my thanks to the following people who worked on the book at Maggid Books: Shira Finson, Ita Olesker, Avichai Gamdani, Adam Bernstein, Sorelle Spitzer, Yonatan Shai Freedman and Rachel Kellner.

In writing this book, I have benefitted from discussions with my children Jacob, Moshe, Chaim, and Hayley, and on occasion have taken their advice – and, of course, that of my wife Anna. The constant encouragement from my wife made my "learning" possible and my plans for this book a reality. As Rabbi Akiva put it, *"Sheli v'shelachem, shelah hi."*

This edition is dedicated to the loving memory of my parents ז״ל. Suffice it to say here that in the war years, when this was not taken for granted even in the most Orthodox circles, my parents arranged for me to spend my summer holidays in yeshivah – and eventually to remain in the yeshivah for several years. For this alone – and for so many other things – my debt to them is beyond words.

Finally, a prayer:

מה אשיב לה׳ כל תגמולוהי עלי... ואני תפילה: יהי רצון מלפניך שלא תמוש התורה מפי ומפי זרעי וזרע זרעי עד עולם.

Introduction

The rabbinic contribution to *Torah sheBe'al Peh* (the Oral Law) is the subtitle and indeed the major concern of this book. The Sinaitic origin of *Torah sheBe'al Peh* – the principle of *Torah min haShamayim* – has been assumed and is the starting point of these investigations. This principle is defined and explained in the chapters of this book, but no attempt has been made to probe or prove its correctness.

There are a great number of writers on this subject who have departed from this principle, while a modern book which deals with the Rabbinic contributions to *Torah sheBe'al Peh* without departing from this principle is hard to come by.

Since the entire Oral Law is from Sinai, how did disputes arise? How did the Sages act when new situations arose that were not provided for in the tradition? To what extent did the Sages enjoy legislative powers? Why are Rabbinic laws binding? Were legal fictions employed to develop Halachah? How did the Mishnah evolve?

These problems are of great importance to anyone who wants to understand what Judaism has to teach, and some of these issues have given rise to great conflicts in our history – such as the schism between the Pharisees and Sadducees some two thousand years ago, down to the conflict between the Orthodox and Reform in our days.

In this book we make it clear that that although the law revealed at Sinai always reigned supreme, the Sages made a massive contribution to its development.

We reject what we call the minimal position, and also the maximal position taken by some modern scholars who are not in the Orthodox tradition. The minimalists make the claim that the Sages never said anything of their own accord. They never did more than pass on traditional teachings which they themselves had received from their masters. They quote *Rishonim* (pre-sixteenth-century Rabbinic authorities) who they claim support this position.

There is indeed a Talmudic saying which might have lent credence to this position. The Gemara states: "R. Elazar said...whoever makes a (halachic) statement he has not heard from his teacher drives the *Shechinah* (Divine Presence) away from Israel" (*Berachot* 27b). The Rosh, however, one of the important *Rishonim* of the thirteenth century, interprets this saying differently. He reads it as if the words in brackets had been part of the text in the following way: "Whoever makes a statement [of his own and claims that he had heard this statement from his teacher whereas in fact] he has not heard [it] from his teacher drives the *Shechinah* away from Israel."

This interpretation is reminiscent of an admonition by the Chasam Sofer to his pupils: "I do not mind if you say *my* Torah [thoughts] in *your* own name, but I very much mind if you say *your* Torah [thoughts] in *my* name."

The maximal position, which we reject even more strongly, claims that the Sages acted as though the Oral Law had been their own property, so that they could do with it whatever they pleased. They added to it and subtracted from it as they saw fit. Particularly, they adapted it to suit the ethos of their own environment and time.

In this book, we show – without going into the polemics (we indulge in polemics in this Introduction only) – that the Sages acted only within the rules and limits laid down by the Sinaitic tradition. Further, that they did not aim to adapt Torah to changing times, but rather to preserve Torah in changing times.

The maximalist often quote the *Pruzbal* (see infra p.117) in aid of their argument. We think the *Pruzbal* lends no support to their claim at all. On the contrary, it is a patent illustration of the aim of the Sages to preserve and reinforce Torah values in changing times.

The *Pruzbal* was a device instituted by Hillel to enable a creditor to continue to collect his debt when it became due, even after a Sabbatical year (*Shemitah*). The Gemara makes it quite clear that Hillel initiated the idea of the *Pruzbal* in order to protect the Torah value of lending money to the poor. There is no suggestion that Hillel felt that the *Shemitah* law was out of keeping with the ethos of his time. The Gemara says that "Hillel instituted the *Pruzbal* because he found that people were not lending money to those in need for fear that the debt would be remitted in a Sabbatical year" (*Gittin* 36a).

In the traditional view the great Rabbinic leaders were, so to speak, partners with God in the creation of *Torah sheBe'al Peh*, just as man is partner with God in developing the physical world. And just as man has to act within the boundaries imposed by the laws of physics in developing the world in which he lives, so the Sages had to act within the limits of Sinaitic law in developing *Torah sheBe'al Peh* which they had received (see Chapter 5). The idea that man can become a partner with God by appropriate interpretation of Torah is a time honored tradition, as the Gemara says: "A judge who tenders a perfectly true halachic decision, becomes a partner with God in creation" (*Shabbat* 10a).

The great eminence to which this elevates the Sages should inspire us to accept their sovereignty even in matters we cannot understand, but it should not deter us in any way from attempting to understand and analyze their works, their words and their methodology.

The Rambam says: "It is appropriate for every man to contemplate the laws of the Holy Torah and to understand their full depths according to his power to do so, and what he does not understand...he must still treat with great respect" (*Hilchot Me'ilah* 8:8).

The work of the Sages can conveniently be classified under two headings: *Interpretation* and *Legislation.* It has been said that interpretation is similar to being asked to continue a story which someone else has started and to finish the story in the spirit of the original storyteller. In contrast, legislation is like telling a completely new story.

Applying this analogy, *mutatis mutandis,* to the Oral Law we can understand that wherever the Sages interpreted the law, the interpretation had the force of Torah law. It is part of the "old story"; it was a discovery of what Torah law had always been. On the other hand, whenever the Sages acted as legislators, they were telling a "new story," and therefore the law had the status of Rabbinic Law only.

In order for the Halachah to say something new, legislation had to be enacted. Thus, it took legislation to prohibit "weighing and measuring" on the Sabbath, although the Torah had already provided the injunction: "On the Sabbath day...you shall do no work" (*Shemot* 20:10). The Sages could not by way of interpretation give the term "work" a meaning it never had before. If "you shall do no work" did not prevent "weighing and measuring" when the Torah was given at Sinai, it could not be interpreted to do so centuries later either.

Interpretation was mostly by means of *svara* – which is normally translated as "logic," but is more accurately described in many cases as "sound judgment," "good sense" or "a moral principle," rather than strict logic.

There can be more than one single conclusion to a given situation as a result of applying "good sense" and "moral judgment"; hence, the Rambam says of interpretation of laws that it is here, and here only, that there can be a dispute between the Sages as to the correct final, legal conclusion. There can be two or more different possible conclusions and the final decision on occasions may turn on a very fine point. *Elu velu divrei Elokim Chayim* – two different views can at times both be "the voice of God." (See Rashi, *Ketubot* 57a, s.v. "*Ko mashma lon.*")

On occasions, interpretation was by means of *drash* – the use of hermeneutic rules of Sinaitic origin. These enabled the Sages to derive laws from the Written Torah. Frequently, however, a law of Sinaitic origin or a law derived by *svara* appear in the Talmud as if it were produced by *drash*. In this case, it is the law that produced the *drash* – not the *drash* that produced the law. This is something which a student would do well to bear in mind when he has difficulty in understanding how a certain *drash* could have produced that particular law. The "why" and "how" of this will be discussed in detail in the relevant chapter of this book.

In addition to their task of interpreting the law and providing new legislation, the Sages had a third task – that of passing on the halachic tradition to future generations.

I would like to suggest that there is a hint of this in the Mishnah (*Avot* 1:1): "The Men of the Great Assembly said three things: Be deliberate in law (*interpretation*), develop many disciples (*pass on tradition*) and make a fence for the Torah (*legislation – Gezerot* and *Takkanot*)."

The Halachic tradition was passed on by word of mouth from teacher to pupil in the form of a concise halachic statement called a *mishnah*. Some early *mishnayot* appear to date back to Biblical times and in any event, according to a persuasive opinion, the basic text of all *mishnayot* was concluded at the latest in the first century. The only things added to the Mishnah thereafter were disputes among the Sages (known as *Tanna'im*) regarding minor issues or details (see pp.139–140). There were several collections of *mishnayot* arranged by different *Tanna'im*. However, it is the arrangement of *mishnayot* by Rabbi Yehudah haNasi at the beginning of the third century which became the standard accepted text, generally referred to as "our Mishnah."

The *mishnayot* were never arranged in the manner of a readily accessible code of law. Mishnah always required the personal teacher-pupil relationship – so that even when the time came that the Oral Law was committed to writing, it remained in a sense *Torah sheBe'al Peh*. The teacher was still indispensable to complete the tapestry of Halachah.

We find an example of this with regard to the Mishnah in *Bava Kama* (3:5): "If A places a jug in the street and B stumbles over it and breaks it, B is not obligated to pay compensation to A." Nothing can be clearer than that statement – or can it? The Talmud asks: "Is B not obliged to look where he is going?" So why is he not liable to pay compensation to A? In answer, the famous Sage of the Talmud, Shmuel, says: "The Mishnah is talking of an accident which happens at night, when it is dark and one cannot see." We would add here that Shmuel is not saying, "I know as an historical fact that this Mishnah was talking about nighttime." Rather, he is saying, "I know it as a halachic fact; for my knowledge of Halachah tells me that this statement is true only if it was speaking of an accident at night."

Questions remain to be asked. Why was the Mishnah, and indeed later the Talmud, never arranged as a more accessible code of law? Why does it not complete a single topic before moving on to the next?

Why does it not start with a general principle and continue from there to consideration of details? Why, in the case of the *mishnah* we have just considered, was a fact that is absolutely crucial omitted in the text, and why does this pattern repeat itself from time to time throughout the Mishnah?

We would suggest that the Sages always preferred that *Torah sheBe'al Peh* should remain a law which could not be mastered on one's own, whether it was studied by rote or from a written text. We would argue that it was left as an incomplete text not, as some might suggest, in order to facilitate fundamental change. Rather, on the contrary, in order to prevent fundamental changes, it required a teacher who could be relied upon to interpret it in the light of the Divine Giver's intent and the Sinaitic tradition.

It was of paramount importance that not only should a teacher be personally involved in passing on a tradition, but that the teacher himself should be of impeccable character, as the Talmud says: "Let the teacher be like an angel of God, and then seek Torah from his mouth" (*Chagigah* 15b).

The need for a teacher, and the exemplary character of the teacher, combine to preserve the authenticity of the tradition, and to give the student the inspiration and vision of greatness without which Torah education is impossible.

The first chapter of this book emphasizes that "part of the Divine Law...was made by men inspired by *ruach hakodesh*," and the last chapter concludes: "...the Mishnah is [described in *Midrash Tanchuma* as] the mystery of God, and God hands over His mysteries only to the righteous."

It is appropriate that our investigation of the Oral Law should have brought us full circle. For that is the nature of all Jewish learning. It is a continuous cycle of constantly returning to where we began. As we say in concluding a volume of the Talmud: *"Hadran alach* – we shall revisit you," as if addressing a good friend from whom it is hard to part.

Chapter 1

The Origin of the Oral Law

INTRODUCTION

The Jewish People are frequently called "the People of the Book"; yet if one were to search out a people who follow the teachings of the Written Law (*Torah sheBichtav*) literally, one might be led to the Samaritans, who still practice their religion on the outskirts of Shechem, or the Karaites, who are now settled to the south of Tel Aviv, but never to the Jewish People. The Jewish People do not now follow the literal word of the Written Law, nor have they ever done so. They have been fashioned and ruled by the verbal interpretation of the written word, more particularly by the Torah, which embraces both the Written and the Oral Law. Rav D.Z. Hoffman writes as follows:[1]

> The Bible word read from the written book and the teachings heard from the mouth of the Sages are for the [Jew] the two sources from which he draws the Torah received by Moshe from God on Sinai. The Torah is one, although the source from which it issues is twofold, the teaching which comes to us from the Mishnah is of identical date and origin as that which is derived

1. *Die Erste Mischna* (Berlin, 1882), p. 3.

> by interpretation of the Scriptural word; all is given by one God and communicated by one and the same prophet. Hence, when we speak of written law and the oral law, we have in mind one and the same law of God derived in part from the Divine word committed to writing and in part from the authoritative statements of the teachers of tradition.

In this short paragraph, Rav Hoffman sets out one of the fundamental propositions of tradition Judaism which we are about to examine, namely that the substance of the Oral Law is of Sinaitic origin. The remainder of this chapter will discuss how, in addition to this substance of the Oral Law that is of Sinaitic origin, there is the Oral Law that the Sages had not received from Sinai which they produced by interpreting the tradition and by creating new legislation. First, however, we must emphasize the Sinaitic origin of the Oral Law, because it is important not to lose sight of the fact that the basic principles of the Oral Law are of Sinaitic origin and that the law which was *made* rather than revealed takes only a secondary place. Indeed, it will be shown how the power of the Sages to make and interpret law stems from the revealed law and is circumscribed by it. The revealed law reigns supreme, notwithstanding the fact that the other law is also part of the Divine Law and was made by men inspired by *ruach hakodesh,*[2(א)*] "so that they shall not err in their judgment."[3]

---

2. **Bava Batra* 12a, *Ramban ad loc.; *Vayikra* 29:4; *Ramban, *Devarim* 17:11; *Divrei Chayim, Yoreh De'ah II,* responsum 105: "Everyone agrees that *ruach hakodesh* did not leave the Sages." Rabbi Yonatan Eibeshutz, **Urim v'Tumim,* quoted by *HaTalmud u'Madai'i HaTevel* (Lvow, 1928), p. 111.
3. *Vayikra Rabbah* 29:4; Chief Rabbi Jakobovits writes: "Judaism never claimed infallibility for its spiritual leaders. *Journal of a Rabbi* (New York, 1966), p. 229. See *Tashbatz* 2:9.

* The full text of all "starred" footnotes is printed in the Hebrew Sources section at the end of each chapter. Hebrew letters in parentheses indicate the notes of Rav Simcha Wasserman, which are found at the end of each chapter.

SECTION I: ORAL LAW OF SINAITIC ORIGIN

It is fortunate that whatever proof there is for the Divine origin of the Torah and the Sinaitic origin of the Oral Law, it is never quite sufficient to be altogether conclusive. Otherwise, the Jews would have lost a faith and an inner conviction and would have gained a mere science as a substitute.

The Written Law Cannot Be Understood Without An Oral Law

Nevertheless, it is possible to show that the Written Law could never have stood alone and that at the same time as the Written Law was given at Sinai, it must have been accompanied by an oral tradition.

Hillel attempted to show this when he was faced by an intending proselyte, who was quite willing to accept the Written Law but would not accept the oral tradition. The Talmud[4] in an *Aggadic* passage relates how Hillel showed him that such an attitude was completely untenable, because without an oral tradition it is not possible even to identify the letters of the *Alef-Bet.*

There are two further arguments of which Hillel might have made use:

1. That it is difficult, if not impossible, to make sense of the Written Law without an oral tradition.
2. That there are principles of Oral Law which date from the same time as the Written Law.

The Necessity for an Oral Tradition

There are countless terms in the Scripture that are undefined – for example the term "work" in sabbatical law, or the term "slaughtering" in *kashrut* law. These are all terms which the Torah uses, but does not define. It does not define what "work"[5] is forbidden or how animals are to be "slaughtered."[6]

---

4. *Shabbat* 31a
5. **Shemot* 31:14.
6. **Devarim* 12:21.

There are basic legal concepts and institutions, the existence of which is assumed by the Torah, but which are not further explained.[7] For example, without previously specifying the formalities of marriage and divorce, the Torah states that a first husband cannot remarry the wife he has divorced, if in the meantime she has been married to another man.[8]

Read without any oral tradition, there are passages in the Bible which appear contradictory. The number of days during which *matzah* (unleavened bread) must be eaten on Pesach is given as seven in *Shemos*[9] but as six in *Devarim*.[10] The Oral Law[11] explains the discrepancy by stating that the six-day period is one during which the eating of unleavened bread is voluntary, as it is equally permissible to eat potatoes or any other food not containing leavened substance. The seven-day period includes the one day (i.e. the first) on which there is a positive duty to eat *matzah*.

What meaning have such contradictory passages, without some oral tradition? Also, the fact that the Torah frequently deals with the exceptional case, rather than with the principles, indicates the reliance on another statement of law – namely the Oral Law. Rabbi Shimshon Raphael Hirsch, the nineteenth century founder of modern German Orthodoxy, in his commentary to the Pentateuch, points out that in the Scripture, civil and criminal law commences with the words, "These are the laws which you shall put before them,"[12] and the Torah immediately proceeds to the laws of slavery. The Torah does not even consider it necessary to begin by stating the laws and principles concerning personal liberty and freedom, because for these principles, complete reliance is placed on the Oral Law.

Principles of the Oral Law from the Time of the Written Law

The Mishnah, too, yields some evidence of the existence of an Oral Law at the very dawn of Jewish history. There are laws contained in *mishnayot*

---

7. See R. Yehudah haLevi, **Kuzari, Maamar* 3, par. 35.
8. **Devarim* 24:1- 4.
9. *Shemot* 12:15.
10. *Devarim* 16:8.
11. *Pesachim* 120a.
12. *Shemot* 21:1.

which have relevance only to a state of affairs which prevailed before the Jews first settled in the Land of Israel.[13] We shall mention two examples:

One *mishnah*[14] deals with leprosy signs which had already appeared upon one of the people *before the Torah was given at Sinai.* It rules that such signs did not render such a person unclean, even after the Torah was given.

Another *mishnah*[15] deals with the cities which were set aside as a refuge for a man who killed by accident. There were three such cities east of the Jordan, and three in the Land of Israel.[ב] The *mishnah* rules that when the Jews first conquered the land east of the Jordan, though they appointed cities of refuge there, these were not operative until all six cities had been designated.

There must already have been an Oral Law in existence at the time of Sinai and when the Jews reached the Jordan; to argue otherwise would mean that these laws were formulated at a time when they no longer applied in practice.

Furthermore, mention should be made of two *mishnayot* which deal with problems that arose when the Israelites first reached the Land of Israel. The problem of *orlah* (which prohibits the free use of the trees until their fifth year), and its effect on these first settlers in Israel is considered by the Mishnah. Did the laws of *orlah* apply to trees that had not been planted by Jews, but were found there when the Land was conquered? The Mishnah[16] rules that *orlah* did not apply, except in the words of the Scripture "when you come to the land and plant."

The problem of the daughters of Zelofechad when they first came to settle in Israel is considered in another *mishnah.* The fact that Zelofechad had no male descendents had already given rise to some problems in Moshe Rabbenu's lifetime,[17] when it was ruled that Zelofechad's property should pass to his daughters. The Mishnah[18]

---

13. The argument developed here and the examples follow Rav Hoffman's *Die Erste Mischna.*
14. *Mishnah *Negaim* 7:1.
15. *Mishnah *Makkot* 2:4.
16. *Mishnah *Orlah* 1:2.
17. See *Bemidbar* 27:1
18. *Mishnah *Bava Batra* 8:3.

states that the daughters of Zelofechad were entitled to the portion of their father and of their grandfather in the Land of Israel. The Land was to be divided according to the entitlement of those who left Egypt (among whom both their father and grandfather were to be counted) and if they were no longer alive, their descendants took their respective shares.[ג]

All these *mishnayot* indicate that the Oral Law existed from the very outset of Jewish history. These *halachot* are almost as old as the Jewish People themselves. No one with an unprejudiced mind would suggest that these *halachot* were produced after the events to which they relate. It is absurd to suggest that some Sages, centuries after the laws were given at Sinai, enacted a law which applied to people who had leprosy signs before the Torah was given. Who could possibly be affected by such an enactment? So, we find an Oral Law in existence at the time of Sinai and at the time when the Israelites reached the promised land.

An Oral Law Must Always Have Existed but What Did It Comprise?

These *mishnayot* show not only that the Oral Law existed at an early date, but also *what* it comprised. The evidence of the Scripture itself, where certain apparent deficiencies indicate that there must have been an Oral Law to complement the text, does not show *what* this Oral Law comprised. Those who subscribe to the traditional view claim that this Oral Law was the *Torah sheBe'al Peh* taught by the Sages. Others – such as the Saducees – were not prepared to accept that the very *Torah sheBe'al Peh* which the Sages taught was the tradition which had always accompanied the Written Law and which had, in fact, been handed down to Moshe by God Himself. They, too, had to admit that there had always been an oral law to explain, expound and supplement the Written Law, but they would argue that the original Oral Law was not one and the same with that taught by the Sages.[ד] For traditional Judaism, however, it has always been one of the fundamental tenets that "the teaching which comes to us from the Mishnah is of identical date and origin as that which is derived by interpretation of the Scriptural word;[ח] all is given by one God and communicated by one and the same prophet."[19]

Talmudic Dicta Concerning the Origin of the Oral Law

The Talmud and Midrash contain a number of statements which affirm that the entire Oral Law – including the Mishnah and the Gemara – originated at Sinai,[20] where it was given by God to Moshe Rabbenu.[21] Moshe knew all that a conscientious student of the Torah would ever produce in the future[22] and when God gave him the Torah, He explained it to him in all its detail.[23]

How do the traditional commentators understand these statements? Rambam,[24] the great eleventh-century philosopher and codifier, claims that, for example, when God gave the laws of *sukkah* to Moshe, He did not only say, "You shall dwell in booths seven days." He added that all men (but no women) are obliged to eat, drink and sleep in the *sukkah;* that the obligation does not apply to those on journeys, or to the sick; that the minimum measurements of the *sukkah* are 7x7x10 *tefachim* (handbreadths) and that certain materials are permissible for constructing the roof, and others are not; and that He gave all the other detailed instructions comprised in the Oral Law.

If this is the case, the question may well be asked: Are not they

---

19. *Die Erste Mischna,* loc. cit.
20. **Berachot* 5a.
21. See *Tradition,* Vol. 9, nos. 1 and 2, where Professor Wyshograd discusses the Orthodox view regarding "revelation" and the form in which God "spoke." We would suggest that when the Torah states that God "spoke," it means that the nearest equivalent in human terms to what took place is "speech," because the Torah makes use of human terms to describe superhuman events.
22. *Kohelet Rabbah* 1:9; **Talmud Yerushalmi, Pe'ah* 2:4; **Megillah* 19b.
23. **Sifra Behar.* See, however, *Shemot Rabbah* 41, where R. Avia asks rhetorically "and did then Moshe learn the entire Torah?" and he replies, "No, God taught him only the principles." Also, *Sefer HaIkkarim* 3:23 states: "It is not possible to claim that God gave the Torah in such a way that it should provide for all times and all events. Moshe was given only the principles, by means of which the sages of future generations deduced the laws applicable to any situation."
24. **Introduction to Seder Zera'im.*

right who claim that the Sages did not make any contribution of their own to the Oral Law?

We shall attempt to answer this question.

SECTION II: ORAL LAW OF RABBINIC ORIGIN

Did the Sages make no contribution to the Oral Law? And was everything they said a mere echo of the tradition they had received at Sinai?

At first sight it may appear that at least two great authorities, Rabbenu Chananel and Ra'avad, assert that the Sages contributed nothing original to the Oral Law.

The View of Rabbenu Chananel

Rabbenu Chananel, a tenth-century Biblical and Talmudic commentator, considers the following Talmudic problem. The Talmud[25] is faced by two apparently contradictory statements:

1. A statement by the second-century *Tanna,*[26] R. Shimon bar Yochai, that those who receive God's Presence are only a few.
2. A statement by the fourth-century *Amora,* Rava, that there are 18,000 who receive God's Presence.

The Talmud accordingly questions the contradiction, "How can R. Shimon say that there are only a few when Rava said there are 18,000 who receive Gods Presence?"

So much for our Talmudic problem. R. Chananel,[27] with whose comments on this we are here concerned, has a different problem. He asks: "How can the Talmud challenge a statement of R. Shimon bar Yochai because it contradicts something said centuries later by another of the Sages? Was he to take into consideration in the second century

25. **Sukkah* 45b.
26. A *Tanna* is a teacher quoted in the Mishnah or *Baraita,* in contradistinction to an *Amora,* a teacher whose discussion on the Mishnah is reported in the Gemara.
27. *Commenting on *Sukkah* 45b.

what Rava would be saying in the fourth century?" To this R. Chananel gives the following answer: The words of Rava "merely record a tradition already known to the rabbis...because these statements and others like them cannot be made except when received through the prophets."

At first this appears to support the view that none of the Sages ever made a statement that they had not received by tradition. However, this cannot be correct because R. Chananel's statement is qualified by the words *"these statements and others like them,"* words which clearly indicate that he is of the view that the Sages *did* make statements of their own accord. "These statements and others like them" are exceptional, because they deal with a celestial mystery – the question of receiving God's Presence. In such matters, the Sages would not speak of their own accord nor say anything that they had not received via the prophets.

The View of Ra'avad

There is one other authority who has to be considered in this connection, namely Ra'avad, the twelfth-century Spanish Talmudist, who writes:[28] "The Sages of the Talmud and certainly those of the Mishnah never said even a small thing of their own accord, except *Takkanot,* which they instituted anonymously, in order to create a fence around the Torah."

Here indeed we would have support for the contention that the Sages never contributed anything new to the Oral Law, were it not for the fact that Ra'avad immediately goes on to say:[29] "The Sages never had any dispute regarding the principle of any mitzvah; their disputes concerned the details only"; and now come the operative words: "They had heard the principles from their teachers, and had not inquired about the details." Clearly then, according to Raavad, a substantial part of the Talmud which deals with the detailed application of the mitzvot comprises statements of the Sages not based on information their teachers had received from Sinai, but based on their own understanding of what the law should be, having regard to the principles they had received from their teachers.

28. **Sefer HaKabbalah* (Jerusalem 1956), p. 1.

29. According to one reading of *Vayikra Rabbah* 32:1. See also *Megillah* 19b.

These two authorities do in fact demonstrate that the Sages contributed views, statements and *halachot* of their own. Indeed the very idea that the entire Oral Law was communicated to Moshe is expressed in the words "Moshe knew all that a conscientious student would produce (*mechadesh*) in future," which indicate further developments of the Law after the time of Moshe. The proposition that the Sages did make original contributions to the Oral Law brings us to another problem: Does this contradict the statement that the entire Oral Law was communicated by God to Moshe at Sinai?

Moshe Did Not Hand Down All the Oral Law He Had Received

There are at least two possible solutions. One is to suggest that although the entire Oral Law was communicated to Moshe at Sinai, Moshe did not pass it all on to future generations. In fact, the *Talmud Yerushalmi*[30] suggests that Moshe was not permitted to pass on the entire Oral Law to others. Accordingly, whereas Moshe received the entire Oral Law at Sinai, he did not communicate it all to Yehoshua, his disciple, because he was not allowed to do so.

Much That Was Taught Was Later Forgotten

Another solution lies in the natural erosion caused by the passage of time.[31] Possibly, in the fullness of time, much that Moshe had passed on was forgotten. The Talmud[32] reports that Yehoshua was made to forget three hundred laws as a punishment for a proud answer he once gave to Moshe. Shortly before his death, Moshe invited him to clear up any doubt which he might have regarding *halachah*. The latter gave the proud answer, "I have no difficulties," and forgot three hundred *halachot* on that

30. **Talmud Yerushalmi, Avodah Zarah* 2:7 and see also *Megillat Esther* on *Sefer HaMitzvot, Shoresh* 1 (note 16) and R. Yom-Tov Lipman, *Introduction to *Tosefot Yom-Tov, Masechet Berachot.*
31. See Chazon Ish, *Collected Letters* (Bnei Brak, 1956), Part II, p. 24: "The Sages produced again what had been forgotten."
32. **Temurah* 16a.

day. Moreover, it would appear that forgetfulness was a penalty exacted from later generations as well, on account of their lack of humility. Had they only had sufficient humility to listen carefully to their elders and diligently absorb their teachings, there would never have been any doubts or controversies regarding the law.[(ו)] As it was, the Talmud reports that the pupils of Hillel and Shammai did not serve their masters as much as was necessary and consequently the number of doubts and controversies increased.[33] The Talmud[34] also reports that their master, Hillel, had made a similar complaint against the leaders of his own generation. Had they only listened sufficiently to Shmaya and Avtalyon,[(ז)] the two great teachers, they would not have been in doubt regarding the *halachah*. It may be assumed that all generations were beset by forgetfulness[35] and consequently, the Oral Law – communicated in its entirety to Moshe at Sinai – was, by the period of the Sages, incomplete. There were many gaps which remained to be filled, and they were filled by the original contributions of the Sages.

The two categories of law – those which originated at Sinai and those made by the Sages – together formed the *Torah sheBe'al Peh* which is part of the Divine law of God. There is a clear distinction in the nature of the two types of law.

Rambam[36] explains that the Oral Law received by the Sages in a direct chain of tradition from Sinai remained for all time clear and certain, free from doubt and controversy, whereas the law which did not come by way of tradition was beset by many disputes; we will discuss this distinction in greater detail.

---

33. *Sanhedrin* 88b, *Sotah* 47b.

34. *Pesachim* 66a.

35. See **Sukkah* 20a and *Yoma* 81a, *Shabbat* 104a, *Sukkah* 44a.

36. *Introduction to Seder Zera'im.*

SECTION III: THE TWO TYPES OF LAW DISTINGUISHED AND THE ORIGIN OF DISPUTES

While the Sanhedrin Functioned There Were No Disputes

No disputes between the Sages were recorded in early times. If any disputes arose which concerned a matter of law, it was soon settled. The Talmud[37] states that all controversies were referred to the Sanhedrin where they were put to the vote. For example, if a question of ritual cleanness was involved then "if the majority voted unclean, they declared it so; if clean, they ruled even so." In the result, as long as the Sanhedrin existed, no disputes were recorded.[38] The Oral Law spoke with a single voice on every issue. No records had to be kept of the different views,[(ח)] because once the Sanhedrin had decided the *halachah*, there was only one view that mattered, namely, that which accorded with the decision of the majority. When, however, political conditions no longer allowed a Sanhedrin to function – in the time of Hillel and Shammai – separate schools arose, each having its own view, and there was no forum in which these disputes could be resolved.[(ט)]

Even After the Sanhedrin Ceased, Sinaitic Law Remained Free from Disputes

However, the position was different regarding Sinaitic laws. The Oral Law which had been transmitted in a chain of tradition from Sinai remained

---

37. *Sanhedrin* 88b.

38. With regard to these early laws, there is only one recorded dispute which remained unsettled. It arose in the following circumstances (*Mishnah *Chagigah* 2:2). Normally, the Torah required a person to lay his hands on his Temple sacrifice (see *Vayikra* 1:4). On the Sabbath and *Yom Tov*, however, the Sages had forbidden the handling of animals. The question then arose whether or not the Rabbinic prohibition against handling animals on *Yom Tov* applied even in this case, when the handling of the animals was required in order to comply with the ritual that the Torah had prescribed for sacrifices. This question divided the Sanhedrin for five generations, the *Nasi* taking the one view and the President of the Court the other. No one can say with certainty why this controversy was not resolved in the same way as the other disputes.

for all time free from controversy and doubt. There was no question of settling disputes, because disputes could never arise. If, in the course of a Talmudic argument, one of the Sages expressed a view that a certain law seemed to him to be open to objection, he would usually take care to add that if that law was based on tradition, he would therefore accept it.[39]

Yet, even without adding this rider, it was understood that a law could not be challenged if it had been received in a direct line of transmission from Sinai, and so such laws remained for all time free from doubt and controversy.

The Classification Adopted by Rambam

What has been said so far is of the greatest importance in the classification adopted by Rambam.[40] For he draws a clear distinction between the two types of law, those which are of Sinaitic origin and which are not subject to controversy, and those not of Sinaitic origin, which are subject to controversy. In this classification, the Sinaitic laws consist of:

1. Interpretations received at Sinai of the Scripture
2. *Halachah l'Moshe miSinai*

Non-Sinaitic laws consist of:

1. Laws derived by the Sages[41]
2. *Takkanot* and *Gezerot*[42]

Problems Concerning Halachah l'Moshe miSinai

More will be said about this classification in the next chapter with particular reference to the non-Sinaitic laws. Here we will add only a few remarks concerning *halachah l'Moshe miSinai.*

39. Mishnah *Negaim* 9:3 and 11:7; *Mishnah *Yevamot* 8:3; Mishnah *Kritot* 3:9.
40. **Introduction to Seder Zera'im.*
41. The Sages derived laws by means of *drash* and logic. See next chapter.
42. See Chapter 3 for *Takkanot* and *Gezerot.*

As Rambam defines this term, it applies to laws which have no intrinsic connection with the Scripture but are of Sinaitic origin. This is its strict technical meaning, although the term is sometimes used more loosely to describe laws which are of long standing, even though they are not of Sinaitic origin.[43]

This definition of Rambam has been much criticized for two reasons. Firstly, according to Rambam, laws of Sinaitic origin are not subject to controversy; yet there are a number of controversies in the Talmud concerning *halachah l'Moshe miSinai.*[44] Secondly, according to Rambam, laws classed as *halachah l'Moshe miSinai* are distinguished by not having any intrinsic connection with the Scripture; yet the Talmud describes certain laws as *halachah l'Moshe miSinai* and still connects them via *midrash* with the Scripture.[45]

---

43. Mishnah *Yadayim* 4:3, *Bartenura,* ad loc.; Rosh, *Introduction to Mikvaot.*
44. See R. Chayim Bachrach in *Chavot Yair,* Responsum 192, who cites many cases of controversy concerning *halachah l'Moshe miSinai.* It seems, however, that disputes in *halachah l'Moshe miSinai* concern only details which do not go to the root of the law. There is no case of *halachah l'Moshe miSinai* where one *Tanna* declares an object kosher or an act permitted and another declares the identical object or act prohibited.
45. *Shabbat* 103b; *Eruvin* 4b. Rambam, Mishnah *Sukkah* 4:9, distinguishes between an open *remez* (allusion) and one that is hidden (or merely an *asmachta*). See also *Megillat Esther* on *Sefer HaMitzvot, Shoresh* 1.

Notes of Rav Simcha Wasserman זצ״ל

א. צריך ביאור כי לא בשמים היא והרמב״ן מתכוין לסיעתא דשמיא.

[הערת העורך: אין כוונת מחה״ס שהם פסקו על פי רוה״ק כעין נבואה אלא שע״י יגיעה בתורה בכל קניניה זוכין לרוה״ק כדי לכוין את ההלכה ואת רצון ה׳ כמבואר בשו״ת חת״ס או״ח סי׳ ר״ח ואגרות חזו״א ח״א סי׳ ל״ג. ונראה שזו גם כוונת הרמב״ן בב״ב דף י״ב.]

ב. אין זו ראיה מוכרחת כי אפשר שלמדו אח״כ מה היה הדין מקודם. מ״מ הוא ראיה שהיה הדין כבר אז.

ג. אין הכרח, הרי ירושת בנות צלפחד נוגעת ליורשיהן. [וא״כ גם אם נקבל טענות רד״צ הופמן באותן משניות שאין להן השלכה מעשית בתקופה יותר מאוחרת, מ״מ משנה זו שנוגעת גם להבא יתכן שהוא מדור מאוחר.]

[הערת העורך: גם רי״א הלוי ז״ל ב״דורות הראשונים״ הפנה טענות אלה שבהערה ב׳ וג׳ אל רד״צ הופמן ז״ל, וע׳ בזה שו״ת שרידי אש ח״ד ע׳ רכ״ה.]

ד. בפיה״מ להרמב״ם בפ״א מאבות מ״ג מתבאר שהצדוקים הראשונים כפרו גם בתורה שבכתב ורק חזרו לאמת אותה בכדי שיתקבלו דבריהם בביטול המסורה ותורה שבע״פ. [מתוך מכתב למחה״ס שנדפס בקובץ מאמרים ואגרות ח״ג ע׳ רצ״ז.]

ה. מדמה משנה לדרשות או דרשות למשנה? [הכוונה להעיר על רד״צ הופמן שמדמה הדרשות דתורה שבכתב למשנה או להיפך, והרי שניהם יסודם מחז״ל ואנו רוצים להוכיח שהמשנה והדרשות ניתנו יחד עם התורה בסיני.] ולקמן בפרק ו׳ מסתפק [מחה״ס] בקידום נוסחת המשנה. [וכל עוד שלא הוכח קידמת המשנה מסיני אין לנו גבוי לקביעותו של רד״צ הופמן.]

[הערת העורך: נראה שכוונת רד"צ הופמן לדמות תוכן המשניות והלכותיה לדינים שנתפרשו להדיא בתורה, ששניהם ניתנו ביחד מרועה אחד בסיני, וכן ממש כתב רי"א הלוי בדורות הראשונים ח"א[ה] עמ' 516 שאין הבדל בין דברי התורה המפורשים "בסוכות תשבו" לבין הקבלה "שאין מסככין בדבר המק"ט", שניהם ניתנו מרועה אחד, ואילו נידון מחה"ס בפ"ו הוא רק עריכת הנוסח.]

ו. טועה בעיקר הענין, והענין שנחלקו רק בסברא מפני חולשת הסברא ולא מפני השכחה. עיין הקדמה לזרעים [פיה"מ להרמב"ם ד"ה אבל אמרם] על הגמ' בסנהדרין דף פ"ח: משרבו תלמידי שמאי והלל שלא שימשו כל צרכם וכו'. [ע"ש שאין להאשימם בכך שלא נתווכחו לפי רמת שכלם של שמאי והלל.]

[הערת העורך: אמת שלא הוזכר כאן שכחה. ועם זה ילה"ע דדברי הרמב"ם אינם מוסכמים, דמחה"ס ציין שגמרא זו הובאה נמי בסוטה דף מ"ז: ולפני כן איתא שם "משרבו זחוחי הלב רבו מחלוקת בישראל", ופרש"י שאין מטין את אזנם לשמוע יפה מפי רבם וסומכים על בינתם.]

ז. הלל אמר מי גרם לכם וכו' שלא שמשתם ב' גדולי הדור, דהיינו גמרא. [הכוונה דמה שאמרו "שלא שמשתם כו'" ענינו הוא מה שנקרא גמרא, דהיינו הבנת טעמי המשניות כמבואר ברש"י ברכות דף ה. ד"ה זה גמרא ודף מ"ז: ד"ה שלא שימש ת"ח וע'

גם רש"י סוטה דף כ"ב. ד"ה שמורין, וא"כ אינו ענין ל"שלא שימשו" המוזכר בסנהדרין דף פ"ח: לפי פיה"מ הנ"ל.]

ח. צ"ע מעדויות פ"א מ"ה למה נזכרו דברי היחיד לבטלן וכו'. [כלומר הרי מבואר במשנה שם כמה תועליות אשר למענם הוזכרו דברי היחיד במשניות. וא"כ מדוע קבע מחה"ס שלא הוצרכו לתעד את הדעות השונות כאשר נחלקו חכמי הסנהדרין.]

[הערת העורך: נראה דבסנהדרין דעת המיעוט בטלה לגמרי, והיחיד חייב לחזור בו ע' רמב"ן על סה"מ שורש א', לעומת מחלוקות אחרות דאף שהוכרעו ג"כ לפי הרוב מ"מ אין זה כח הרוב דאורייתא כיון שלא עמדו למנין במושב אחד כמבואר בגט פשוט בסוה"ס כלל א. ולכן בשעהד"ח סומכין על יחיד כשלא איתמר הלכתא להדיא כהרוב ע' ט"ז יו"ד סי' רצ"ג סק"ד וכ"כ באו"ז סוכה סי' ש"ו עפ"י מתני' דעדויות. מיהו הש"ך שם סוס"י רמ"ב נקט שאפי' לא נחלקו במושב אחד פא"פ אלא כמחל' התנאים ואמוראים והפוסקים, הלכה כהרוב מה"ת, וסובר דבדאו' אף בשעה"ד א"א לסמוך על היחיד דהוא כאיתמר הלכתא, ולדבריו הדרה קושית הרש"ו.]

ט. היה סנהדרין לילך אחר הרוב אלא שלא נשאלה הלכה למעשה, וצ"ע בעובדא

דיוחנן החורני סוכה כ"ח. וכו' [ששם היה הנידון למעשה ועכ"ז נשארו זקני ב"ש וב"ה בויכוח]. וגם לא היה אפשר לילך אחר הרוב משום דב"ש מחדדי טפי, עיין יבמות י"ד.

[הערת העורך: ב"יסוד המשנה ועריכתה" להרב ר. מרגליות ז"ל עמוד ח' הוכיח שהרומיים ביטלו בי"ד הגדול [ע' רמב"ם פ"א מממרים ה"ד] מטעמים מדיניים וכאשר תיפקודו התאפשר מחדש נתעוררה השאלה מי ראוי למנות ולהמנות ולכן נתחלקו לבתי מדרש שונים. ובסוף דבריו הזכיר ג"כ שלא היו יכולים לעמוד למנין, דבית הלל לכל אדם שנו ובכן היו גדולים במנין, ואילו בית שמאי היו חריפי טפי.]

Hebrew Sources

SECTION I

Ruach Hakodesh Inspired the Sages in Their Law-Making

2.* *Bava Batra 12a*

אמר רבי אבדימי דמן חיפה, מיום שחרב בית המקדש ניטלה נבואה מן הנביאים וניתנה לחכמים.

2. *Ramban, ad loc.*

הכי קאמר אעפ״י שנטלה נבואת הנביאים שהוא המראה והחזון, נבואת החכמים שהיא בדרך החכמה לא נטלה, אלא יודעים האמת ברוח הקדש שבקרבם.

2. *Ramban, Devarim 17:11*

אפילו יהיה בעיניך כ(אילו החכם) מחליף הימין בשמאל, וכל שכן שיש לך לחשוב שהם אומרים על ימין שהוא ימין. כי רוח השם על משרתי מקדשו, ולא יעזוב את חסידיו לעולם נשמרו מן הטעות ומן המכשול.

2. *Rabbi Yonatan Eibeshutz, Urim vTumim*

מרן הגאון הרבי ר׳ יונתן זצ״ל בספרו ״אורים ותומים״ יאמר, דמה שמוכיחים לפעמים איזה דין מחודש ואיזה סברא חדשה מדברי חז״ל מדמשני הכי, ולא משני באופן אחר, שמע מינה דאין הדין כן כמו שנראה מאופן האחר שעלה בדעתנו ליישב, כל זה הוא מפני שהתלמוד ברוח הקודש נאמר, ואילו היה אפשר לתרץ באופן זה בודאי היו מרגישים גם המה מזה האופן, ואם חז״ל לא הביאו אופן זה ותירצו באופן האמור בגמרא, זה האות שהאופן שלנו שעלה בדעתנו לא נכון הוא ואינה לאמיתה של תורה.

* The numbers correspond to the revelant footnotes.

Terms Which Are Not Defined in the Torah

5. Shemot 31:14

ושמרתם את השבת כי קדש הוא לכם מחלליה מות יומת כי כל העשה בה מלאכה ונכרתה הנפש ההוא מקרב עמיה.

6. Devarim 12:21

כי ירחק ממך המקום אשר יבחר ה׳ אלוקיך לשום שמו שם וזבחת מבקרך ומצאנך אשר נתן ה׳ לך כאשר צויתך. ואכלת בשעריך בכל אות נפשך.

7. R. Yehudah haLevi, Kuzari, Ma'amar 3, par. 35

אמר הכוזרי: כן אומרים הקראים אבל אחר שמצאו התורה שלמה אינם צריכים אל הקבלה.

אמר החבר: ...התראה כאשר אמר להם: החדש הזה לכם ראש חדשים על הדמיון לא נסתפק העם אם רצה לומר: חדשי המצרים שהיו ביניהם או חדשי כשדים שהיו עם אברהם באור כשדים, או רצה חדשי השמש או חדשי הירח... ומה ענין הזביחה ושמא היא נחירה או הרג...

והייתי רוצה שיבאר לי החלב האסור והוא דבר עם המותר במעים והקיבה.

...והייתי רוצה שיבאר לי העוף הטהור מן הטמא, זולת המפורסמים, רצוני לומר: בן יונה או תור, ומאין הוא אומר שאין התרנגולת והאוז והקורא ואלברכיה מהטמאים. והייתי רוצה שיתן לי גבול, אל יצא איש ממקומו ביום השבת, אם הוא ביתו או חצירו או רשותו...

8. Devarim 24:1–4

כי יקח איש אשה ובעלה והיה אם לא תמצא חן בעיניו כי מצא בה ערות דבר וכתב לה ספר כריתת ונתן בידה ושלחה מביתו. ויצאה מביתו והלכה והיתה לאיש אחר. ושנאה האיש האחרון וכתב לה ספר כריתת ונתן בידה ושלחה מביתו או כי ימות האיש האחרון אשר לקחה לו לאשה. לא יוכל בעלה הראשון אשר שלחה לשוב לקחתה להיות לו לאשה אחרי אשר הטמאה כי תועבה הוא לפני ה׳ ולא תחטיא את הארץ אשר ה׳ א׳ נתן לך נחלה.

Old Laws in the Mishnah

14. Mishnah Negaim 7:1

אלו בהרות טהורות. שהיו בו קודם למתן תורה. (מי שהיתה בו צרעת קודם מתן

תורה לא היה טמא מחמת אותו נגע לאחר מתן תורה. (ר"ע מבטרנורה).

15. Mishnah Makkot 2:4

להיכן גולין, לערי מקלט. לשלש שבעבר הירדן ולשלש שבארץ כנען. שנאמר (במדבר ל"ה) את שלש הערים תתנו מעבר לירדן ואת שלש הערים תתנו בארץ כנען וגו׳.

עד שלא נבחרו שלש שבארץ ישראל, לא היו שלש בעבר הירדן קולטות.

16. Mishnah Orlah 1:2

עת שבאו אבותינו לארץ מצאו נטוע פטור, נטעו אע"פ שלא כבשו חייב.

18. Mishnah Bava Batra 8:3

בנות צלפחד נטלו שלשה חלקים בנחלה. חלק אביהן שהיה עם יוצאי מצרים וחלקו עם אחיו בנכסי חפר ושהיה בכור נוטל שני חלקים.

The Entire Oral Law Originated at Sinai

20. Berachot 5a

וא"ר לוי בר חמא אמר ר׳ שמעון בן לקיש, מאי דכתיב "ואתנה לך את לוחות האבן והתורה והמצוה אשר כתבתי להורותם". "לוחות" אלו עשרת הדברות, "תורה" זה מקרא, "והמצוה" זו משנה, "אשר כתבתי" אלו נביאים וכתובים, להורותם" זה גמרא, מלמד שכולם נתנו למשה מסיני.

22. Talmud Yerushalmi, Pe'ah 2:4

מקרא, משנה, תלמוד ואגדה, אפי׳ מה שתלמיד ותיק עתיד להורות לפני רבו כבר נאמר למשה בסיני.

22. Megillah 19b

מלמד שהראהו הקב"ה למשה דקדוקי תורה ודקדוקי סופרים ומה שהסופרים עתידין לחדש.

23. Sifra Behar

וידבר ה׳ אל משה בהר סיני לאמר מה ענין שמיטה אצל הר סיני והלא כל המצות נאמרו מסיני, אלא מה שמטה שנאמרו כללותיה ודקדוקיה מסיני, אף כולם נאמרו כללותיהם ודקדוקיהם מסיני.

24. Rambam, Introduction to Seder Zera'im

והנה לך משל: הקדוש ברוך הוא אמר למשה: בסכת תשבו שבעת ימים (ויקרא כ"ג מ"ב) אחר כן הודיע שהסכה הזאת חובה על הזכרים לא על הנקבות. ושאין החולים חייבין בה ולא הולכי דרך ושלא יהיה סכוכה אלא בצמח הארץ ולא יסככנה בצמר ולא במשי ולא בכלים אפילו מאשר תצמיח הארץ כגון הכסתות והכרים והבגדים. והודיע שהאכילה והשתיה והשינה בה כל שבעה - חובה; ושלא יהיה בחללה פחות משבעה טפחים ארך על שבעה טפחים רוחב; ושלא יהיה גובה הסכה פחות מעשרה טפחים.

SECTION II

The Sages Contributed Statements and Halachot of Their Own Accord

25. Sukkah 45b

ואמר חזקיה א"ר ירמיה משום רשב"י ראיתי בני עלייה והן מועטין אם אלף הן אני ובני מהן. אם מאה הן אני ובני מהן. אם שנים הן אני ובני הן. ומי זוטרי כולי האי?

והא אמר רבא תמני סרי אלפי דרא הוה דקמיה קודשא בריך הוא שנאמר "סביב שמנה עשר אלף" (יחזקאל מ"ח) לא קשיא הא דמסתכלי באספקלריא המאירה הא דלא מסתכלי באספקלריה המאירה. ודמסתכלי באספקלריא המאירה מי זוטרי כולי האי? והא אמר אביי לא פחות עלמא מתלתין ושיתא צדיקי דמקבלי אפי שכינה בכל יום?

27. Rabbenu Chananel, ad loc.

והלא אביי ורבא דאחרונים הן לגבי רשב"י ואיך מקשינן מדבריהם עליו? אלא ללמדך המסורת שהיה בידם בדברי אביי ורבא כך היה בידי הראשונים בקבלה כהל"מ. ואינם דבריהם, שאלו הדברים וכיוצא בהן אי אפשר להאמר אלא בקבלה מן הנביאים ואלו הדברים שקיבלו מרבותיהם היו מגידין.

28. Ra'avad, Sefer HaKabbalah

זה ספר הקבלה כתבנוהו להודיע לתלמידים כי כל דברי רבותינו ז"ל חכמי המשנה והתלמוד כולם מקובלים חכם גדול וצדיק מפי חכם גדול וצדיק. ראש ישיבה וסייעתו מפי ראש ישיבה וסיעתו מאנשי כנסת הגדולה שקבלו מהנביאים זכר כולם לברכה.

ולעולם חכמי התלמוד וכל שכן חכמי המשנה אפילו דבר קטן לא אמרו מלבם חוץ מן התקנות שתקנו בהסכמת כולם כדי לעשות סייג לתורה.

ואם לחשך אדם לומר מפני שנחלקו בכמה מקומות לכך אני מסופק בדבריהם אף אתה הקהה את שיניו והודיעהו שהוא ממרה על פי בי״ד ושלא נחלקו רז״ל לעולם בעיקר מצוה אלא בתולדותיה מפני שלא שמשו כל צרכן. כיוצא בו לא נחלקו אם מדליקין נר בשבת או לא ועל מה נחלקו במה מדליקין ובמה אין מדליקין.

Moshe Rabbenu Did Not Communicate the Entire Oral Law

30. Talmud Yerushalmi, Avodah Zarah 2:7

א״ר יצחק כתיב ״ואותי צוה ה׳״ (דברים ד׳) אותי ואותי נאמר לי דברים שנאמר לכם ונאמר לי דברים שנאמר בינו לבין עצמי.

30. R. Yom-Tov Lipman, Introduction to Tosefot Yom-Tov, Masechet Berachot

אבל תועלת חבור המשנה וסיבתה היתה לפי שתורה שבע״פ שמסרה משה ליהושע ויהושע לזקנים וכו׳ אע״פ שהיתה ביאור התורה ומצותיה ביאור שלם. אין לך זמון ודור שלא יתחדש בהכרח ויפלא למשפט. ואל תשיבני דבר ממה שאמרו בפ״ב דמגילה (יט:) מאי ועליהם ככל הדברים וכו׳. מלמד שהראהו הקב״ה למשה דקדוקי תורה ודקדוקי סופרים ע״כ. שאני אומר שזה לא היה מוסר משה לאחרים כלל. ודקדוק לשונם כך הוא שאמרו מלמד שהראהו ולא אמר שמסר לו או שלמדו.

In The Fullness of Time Much Law Was Forgotten

32. Temurah 16a

אמר רב יהודה אמר רב: בשעה שנפטר משה רבנו לגן עדן אמר לו ליהושע שאל ממני כל ספקות שיש לך אמר לו רבי כלום הנחתיך שעה אחת והלכתי למקום אחר לא כך כתבת בי ״ומשרתו יהושע בן נון נער לא ימיש מתוך האהל (שמות ל״ג)״ מיד תשש כחו של יהושע ונשתכחו ממנו שלש מאות הלכות ונולדו לו שבע מאות ספיקות...

במתניתין תנא אלף ושבע מאות קלין וחמורין וגזירות שוות ודקדוקי סופרים נשתכחו בימי אבלו של משה. אמר רבי אבהו אעפ״כ החזירן עתניאל בן קנז מתוך פלפולו.

35. Sukkah 20a

שבתחילה כשנשתכחה תורה מישראל עלה עזרא מבבל ויסדה, חזרה ונשתכחה עלה הלל הבבלי ויסדה, חזרה ונשתכחה עלו רבי חייא ובניו ויסדוה.

SECTION III

In Early Times No Disputes Between the Sages Were Recorded

37. Sanhedrin 88b

אמר ר׳ יוסי מתחילה לא היו מרבין מחלוקת בישראל. אלא בית דין של שבעים ואחד יושבין בלשכת הגזית ושני בתי דינין של עשרים ושלושה אחד יושב על פתח הר הבית ואחד יושב על פתח העזרה ושאר בתי דינין של עשרים ושלשה יושבין בכל עיירות ישראל הוצרך הדבר לשאל שואלין מבית דין שבעירן אם שמעו אמרו להן ואם לאו באין לזה שסמוך לעירן אם שמעו אמרו להם ואם לאו באין לזה שעל פתח הר הבית אם שמעו אמרו להם ואם לאו באין לזה שעל פתח העזרה, ואומר כך דרשתי וכך דרשו חברי כך למדתי וכך למדו חברי אם שמעו אמרו להם ואם לאו אלו ואלו באין ללשכת הגזית, ששם יושבין מתמיד של שחר עד תמיד של בין הערבים ובשבתות ובימים טובים יושבין בחיל. נשאלה שאלה בפניהם אם שמעו אמרו להם ואם לאו עומדין למנין רבו המטמאים טמאו רבו המטהרין טהרו. משרבו תלמידי שמאי והלל שלא שמשו כל צרכן רבו מחלוקת בישראל ונעשית תורה כשתי תורות.

The Only Recorded Dispute Which Remained Unsettled

38. Mishnah Chagigah 2:2

יוסי בן יעזר אומר שלא לסמוך. יוסי בן יוחנן אומר לסמוך. יהושע בן פרחיה אומר שלא לסמוך. ניתאי הארבלי אומר לסמוך. יהודה בן טבאי אומר שלא לסמוך. שמעון בן שטח אומר לסמוך. שמעיה אומר לסמוך. אבטליון אומר שלא לסמוך.

הלל ומנחם לא נחלקו. יצא מנחם נכנס שמאי, שמאי אומר שלא לסמוך. הלל אומר לסמוך. הראשונים היו נשיאים ושניים להם אבות בית דין.

A Law Based on Tradition Was Always Accepted

39. Mishnah Yevamot 8:3

עמוני ומואבי אסורים. ואיסורן איסור עולם. אבל נקבותיהם מותרת מיד. מצרי

ואדומי אינם אסורים אלא עד שלושת דורות אחד זכרים ואחד נקבות. רבי שמעון מתיר את הנקבות מיד. אמר רבי שמעון קל וחומר הדברים. ומה אם במקום שאסר את הזכרים איסור עולם התיר את הנקבות מיד. מקום שלא אסר את הזכרים אלא עד ג׳ דורות אינו דין שנתיר את הנקבות מיד. אמרו לו אם הלכה נקבל ואם לדין יש תשובה.

The Classification of Rambam

40. Rambam, Introduction to Seder Zeraim

החלק הראשון - פרושים מקובלים מפי משה ויש להם רמז בכתוב, ואפשר להוציאם בדרך סברא - וזה אין בו מחלוקת אבל כשיאמר האחד "כך קבלתי" - אין לדבר עליו.

החלק השני - הדינים שנאמר בהם: "הלכה למשה מסיני" ואין ראיות עליהם כמו שזכרנו, וזה כמו כן - אין חולק עליו.

החלק השלישי - הדינין שהוציאו על דרכי הסברא ונפלה בם מחלקת, כמו שזכרנו, ונפסק הדין בהם על פי הרב. וזה יקרה - כשישתנה העיון. ומפני כך אומרים: "אם הלכה - נקבל, ואם לדין - יש תשובה". אבל, נפלה המחלוקת והעיון בדבר שלא נשמע בו הלכה. ותמצא בכל התלמוד שהם חוקרים על טעם הסברא שהוא גורם המחלוקת בין החולקים ואומרים: " במאי קא מפלגי"? או "מאי טעמא דרבי פלוני? או"מאי ביניהו"? והם מביאם אותו על ענין זה ברב מקומות, וזוכרים הטעם הגורם למחלקת, כגון שיאמרו: רבי פלוני מחזיק טענה פלונית, ולפלוני מחזיק טענה פלונית וכדומה לו.

אבל מי שיחשוב: שהדיינים שנחלקים בהם, כמו כן מקובלים מפי משה וחושבים שנפלה המחלקת מדרך טעות ההלכות, או השכחה, או מפני שאחד מהם קיבל קבלת אמת והשני טעה בקבלתו, או שכח או לא שמע מפי רבו כל מה שצריך לשמוע: ויביא ראיה על זה ממה שאמרו: "משרבו תלמידי שמאי והלל שלא שמשו כל צרכם, רבתה המחלוקת בישראל ונעשית תורה כשתי תורות" - דברים כאלה הם, חי נפשי, דברים מגונים ומכוערים מאד, והנם דברי מי שאין לו ידיעה ואין בידו העיקרים, ופוגם באנשים אשר נתקבלו מהם

המצוות - וכל זה שוא ובטל. ומה שהביאו להאמין באמונה הזאת הנפסדת הוא: מעוט הסתכלותו בדברי החכמים הנמצאים בתלמוד. שהם מצאו: שכל הפרוש מקובל מפי משה והוא אמת; ולא נתנו הפרש בין "העקרים המקובלים" ובין תולדות הענינים שיוציאו אותם בעיון. אבל, אתה, אל יכנס בלבך ספק במחלוקת בית שמאי ובית הלל באמרם: "מכבדין את הבית ואחר כך נוטלים לידים: או נוטלים לידים ואחר כך מכבדין את הבית", ותחשוב שאחד משני הדברים האלו אינו מקובל מפי משה מסיני - אבל הטעם שהוא גורם להיות חולקים, הוא מה שנזכר בתלמוד: שאחד

מהם אוסר להשתמש בעם הארץ והשני מתיר. וכן כל מה שידמה לאלו החלוקות שהם ענפים מענפי הענפים.

אבל מה שאמרו: "משרבו תלמידי שמאי והלל שלא שמשו כל צרכם רבתה מחלוקת בישראל" ענין זה מבואר: שכל שני אנשים בהיותם שוים בשכל ובעיון ובידיעת "העיקרים" שיוציאו מהם הסברות, לא תפול ביניהם מחלוקת בסברתם בשום פנים, ואם נפלה - תהיה מעוטה, כמו שלא נמצא שנחלקו שמאי והלל אלא בהלכות יחדיות, וזה - מפני שדעות שניהם היו קרובות זו לזו בכל מה שהוציאו בדרך סברא. והעיקרים, כמו כן, הנתונים לזה כמו העיקרים הנתונים לזה. אבל כאשר רפתה שקידת התלמידים על החכמה ונחלשה סברתם כנגד סברת הלל ושמאי רבותיהם - נפלה מחלוקת ביניהם בעיון שעל דברים רבים שסברת כל אחד ואחד מהם היתה לפי שכלו ולפי מה שיש בידו מן העיקרים. ואין להאשימם בכל זאת - שלא נכריח אנחנו לשני חכמים מתוכחים בעיון להתוכח בשכל יהושע ופנחס. ואין לנו ספק כמו כן המה שנחלקו בו, מאחר שאינם כמו שמאי והלל, או כמי שהוא למעלה מהם - שהקדוש ברוך הוא לא צונו בעבודתו על ענין זה, אבל צונו לשמוע מחכמי הדור, כמו שאמר: ואל השופט אשר יהיה בימים ההם (דברים יז, ט). ועל הדרכים האלו נפלה המחלוקת, לא מפני שטעו בהלכות ושהאחד אומר אמת, והשני - שקר. ומה מאד מבואר ענין זה לכל המסתכל בו, ומה יקר וגדול זה העיקר במצוות!

והחלק הרביעי - הם הדינים שתקנו הנביאים והחכמים בכל דור ודור, כדי לעשות סיג וגדר לתורה. ועליהם צוה הקדוש ברוך הוא לעשותם, מה שאמר במאמר כללי: ושמרתם את משמרתי (ויקרא יח, ל), ובאה בו הקבלה: "עשו משמרת למשמרתי". והחכמים יקראו אותם: "גזרות". ולפעמים תפול בהם מחלוקת - לפי שחכם אחד ראה לגזור כך, ולא יסכים עליו חכם אחד. וזה הרבה בתלמוד שאומרים: רבי פלוני גזר כך משום כך וכך, ורבי פלוני לא גזר. וזה כמו כן סיבה מסיבות המחלוקות. שהרי בשר עוף בחלב היא גזירה מדרבנן, כדי להרחיק מן העבירה, ולא נאסר בתורה אלא בשר בהמה טהורה; אבל אסרו חכמים בשר עוף - כדי להרחיק מן האיסור. ויש מהם מי שלא יגזרו גזירה זו: שרבי יוסי הגלילי היה מתיר בשר עוף בחלב, וכל אנשי עירו היו אוכלים אותו, כמו שנתפרסם בתלמוד. וכשתפול הסכמה על אחת מן הגזירות - אין חולקין עליה בשום פנים, וכשיהיה איסורה פשוט בכל ישראל - אין לחלוק על הגזירה ההיא. ואפילו הנביאים בעצמם לא היו רשאים לבטל אותה. וכן אמרו בתלמוד: "שאליהו, זכור לטוב, לא היה יכול לבטל אחד משמונה עשר דבר שגזרו בית שמאי ובית הלל. והביאו טעם על זה: "לפי שאיסורם פשט בכל ישראל".

והחלק החמישי - הם הדינים העשויים על דרך החקירה וההסכמה בדברים הנוהגים בין בני אדם, שאין בם תוספת במצוה ולא גרעון; או בדברים שהם תועלת לבני אדם בדברי תורה, וקראו אותם: "תקנות ומנהגים", ואסור לעבור עליהם.

וכבר אמר שלמה, עליו השלום, על העובר עליהם: ופורץ גדר ישכנו נחש (קהלת י ח). ואלו התקנות רבות מאד ונזכרות בתלמוד ובמשנה: מהן - בענין איסור והתר, ומהן - בענין הממונות: ומהן - תקנות שתיקנו נביאים, כמו תקנות משה ויהושע ועזרא, כמו שאמרו: "משה תיקן להם לישראל שיהיו שואלים ודורשים בהלכות פסח בפסח". ואמרו: "משה תיקן 'הזן' בשעה שירד המן לישראל". אבל תקנות יהושע ועזרא הן רבות. ומהן - תקנות מיוחסות ליחידים מן החכמים, כמו שאמרו: "התקין הלל פורזבול", "התקין רבן גמליאל הזקן", התקין רבן יוחנן בן זכאי". והרבה בתלמוד: "התקין רבי פלוני", "התקין רבי פלוני". ויש מהן תקנות מיוחסות להמון החכמים כמו שאמרו: "באושא התקינו", או כמו שאמרו: "תקנו חכמים" או "תקנות חכמים" וכדומה לזה הרבה.

Chapter 2

Laws Derived by Rabbinic Interpretation

INTRODUCTION

As we have seen[1] the Rambam divides non-Sinaitic laws into groups, as follows:

> GROUP 1. Laws based on *drash* and *svara* (logic or moral reasoning)
> GROUP 2. *Gezerot & Takkanot*[2]

In this chapter we discuss *svara* as logic only. Interpretation by way of moral reasoning is quite an expansive subject and we have given it a place of its own in the following chapter.

We shall first give some examples of laws based on *svara*, or logic. We shall then define "*drash*" and give some examples of laws based on

---

1. See p. 13.
2. The classification of the Oral Law by Rambam has halachic significance. From the point of view of Halachah, laws in any one group are different from laws in another group. See Introduction to *Kiryat Sefer* and Rav Kalman Kahane, *Cheker V'iyun* (Tel Aviv, 1960), Vol. I, p .32.

"*drash*." Finally, we shall consider the binding force of laws based on *drash* and *svara*.

SECTION I: LAWS BASED ON LOGIC

Logic in Delegated Legislation

Some questions were specifically delegated to the Sages by the Torah, so that they should decide them by the use of logic: for example, what "work" was to be prohibited during *Chol haMo'ed*, the intermediate days of a Festival,[3] and what abnormality in an animal was to make it *trefah*,[4] were questions specifically referred to the decision of the Sages.[(א)] In such cases,[5] the Sinaitic law merely propounded the principle – that certain works were to be prohibited during *Chol haMo'ed*, or that certain abnormalities were to make an animal *trefah* – and left it to the Sages to work out the details.

Logic in Rabbinic Interpretations

There are also instances where the Sages deduced laws by means of logic, although the problems were not specifically referred to them by the Torah.[(ב)]

For example, the Talmud states that the law which prohibits the carrying of an object from a public domain into a private domain on the Shabbath is based on a verse in the Scripture. The carrying of an object in the opposite direction, from a private domain into a public domain, is prohibited on the logical ground that there should be no difference between carrying in one direction and carrying in the other.[6(ג)]

3. *Chagigah* 18a; see *Bet Yosef, Orach Chayim* 530 that this is *d'Oraita* contra *Tosafot*, ad loc. See also**Shnei Luchot HaBrit* (*Shlah*), *Torah sheBe'al Peh*.
4. R. Yonaton Eibeshutz, **Kreti, Yorah De'ah, Trefut* 29 (1:5).
5. There are other such cases; see Netziv, *Haamek She'eilah* 47(1) regarding *Muktzeh*; and *R. Nissim (Ran), Mishnah *Yoma* 1:1, regarding washing and wearing shoes on Yom Kippur.
6. **Shabbat* 96b.

Principles of Law Based on Logic

Some of the basic principles of the law, particularly of civil law, are founded upon logic. These principles include the presumption of *Chazakah*[7] and that of *Miggo*.[8(ד)]

SECTION II: LAWS BASED ON *DRASH*

The Purpose and Nature of Drash

What has been said regarding the nature of laws based on logic applies equally to the laws based on *drash*. In these laws, too, the Sages were interpreting the intention of the Torah. Here they made use not of "logic,"[(ה)] but of hermeneutic rules which had been received at Sinai,[9] and perhaps of other rules of language with which they were familiar.[10] *Drash* is by definition an interpretation of a Biblical passage. It is, however, an interpretation which is not in accordance with the plain meaning of the passage. For example, the Biblical verse, "the fathers shall not be put to death on account of the children, nor shall the children be put to death on account of the fathers,"[11] simply means that the sins of the fathers shall not be visited upon the children and vice versa.[12] By means of *drash*, however, the Sages[13] have derived a rule from this verse that certain relatives are not admissible to give evidence, as if "on account of" meant "by the evidence of."[(ו)] Because these interpretations do not

7. Legal presumptions, e.g. that possesion indicates ownership (*Bava Metzia* 100a, *Ketubot* 20a); that one does not pay a debt before the due date (*Bava Batra* 5b); that an agent will carry out his instruction (*Eruvin* 31b, *Gittin* 64a).
8. Presumption that a statement by a witness is true, because had he intended to lie, he could have invented a much more plausible story. See *Bava Batra* 33a, Mishnah *Ketubot* 2:3.
9. Rashi, *Chullin* 16a, s.v. *"Aval"*
10. See p. 33 regarding the view of Malbim. R. Yehudah haLevi (*Kuzari Ma'amar* 3, par. 73) writes: "They either employed secret methods of interpretation, which we do not know, which were handed down to them together with the thirteen *middot* or..."
11. *Devarim* 24:16.
12. See Ramban, *Vayikra* 28:29.
13. *Sanhedrin* 27b.

follow the plain meaning of Biblical passages, nor the rules of logic, it is important to stress that they follow rules of construction and of language which the Sages had received by way of tradition.

Drash Used to Connect Laws of Sinaitic Origin to the Scripture

It is of even greater importance to appreciate that in many cases what appears as *drash* is not a creation of a new law at all, but a mere connecting of the Oral Law to the Scripture where the law is of Sinaitic origin[14] or has its origin in logic[15] or even is itself of Rabbinic origin.[16] In these cases, the fact that the *drash* is not in accordance with the plain or logical meaning of the texts is of no great significance, because the *drash* itself did not create the laws, but on the contrary, the laws created the *drash*.[17] Frequently, it is difficult to ascertain from the Talmud whether a particular *drash* is "creative" or not, in the sense mentioned previously.[18]

In some cases, however, it is self evident that the *drash* is not creative and came after, rather than produced, the law. The case of the *etrog* may serve as an example. The Torah states: "But on the fifteenth day of the seventh month... And on the first day you shall take for yourselves the fruit of a goodly tree."[19] The Talmud[20] "deduces" by means of a *drash* that "a goodly tree" is an *etrog* tree. However, it is obvious that this law was known long before the *drash* was ever made. How otherwise was

14. See Rambam, *Sefer HaMitzvot* (*Shoresh* 2), cited on p. 46, ante. See also Rambam's **Introduction to Seder Zeraim; *Ohr HaChayim* (R. Chayim Ibn Attar), *Vayikra* 13:34.
15. *Kiddushin* 57b; see Rashi, ad loc., s.v. *"Rava."* See also *Shabbat* 135a, *Tosafot*, ad loc., s.v. *"Vela"; *Sanhedrin* 78a; *Kitvei Maharal miPrague* (Jerusalem, 1960), Vol. II, p. 284.
16. This subject is discussed at great length by R' I.I. Halevy, *Dorot HaRishonim* 1:5, p. 467 et seq.
17. The correct term for *drash* which is not "creative" is *"asmachta"* although, as in this chapter, the term *drash* is sometimes used to cover both creative *drash* and *asmachta*.
18. For example, Mishnah *Yevamot* 8:3 quoted on p. 23–24. In some cases, the Talmud, however, states expressly that a *drash* is *asmachta* and that the law is of Sinaitic origin; see also *Eruvin* 4b, *Sukkah* 28a, *Pesachim* 81b, *Ta'anit* 17b, *Niddah* 32a. See also *Chagigah* 4a and *Yevamot* 21a, where the Talmud expressly states that a *drash* is *asmachta* and that the law is of Rabbinic origin.
19. *Vayikra* 23:39-40.
20. *Sukkah* 35b.

the law fillfilled throughout the centuries that had passed between the giving of the Torah at Sinai and the Talmudic era? Evidently, therefore, this is an example of *drash* being used to connect a Sinaitic law to Scripture, and not in order to produce a new law.

Similarly, the Talmud[21] "deduced" by means of *drash* that for the purpose of *shechitah* (ritual slaughter) an animal's throat has to be cut. The Talmud[22] also "deduced" by means of *drash* that *tefillin* must contain four scrolls. These are among the many examples of laws which are clearly of Sinaitic origin and where the *drash* serves no other purpose than to connect well-established law to Scripture.[23]

Drash Used to Connect Laws of Rabbinic Origin to the Scripture

A *ba'al keri* (one who has seminal issue) is forbidden to study Torah. In reply to the question "How do we know that a *ba'al keri* is forbidden to study Torah?" the Talmud in *Masechet Berachot*[24] produces a *drash* based on Scripture. Yet the law that a *ba'al keri* must not study Torah is one of the *Takkanot* of Ezra[25] and not, in fact, a law based on the Torah.

A place of idol worship is ritually unclean. An entire page of Talmud[26] is devoted to a discussion as to why the law declaring such a place ritually unclean is derived from one verse in the Bible in preference to another. Yet on the following page, the Talmud states that the uncleanness attached to a place of idol worship is the result of a Rabbinic decree.

The Purpose of Drash Where It Did Not "Create" Laws

All these cases are instances of *drash* produced by laws; the *drash* was created because the laws were there. Many theories have been advanced to explain the purpose that such *drash* was intended to serve. It has been

21. *Chullin* 27a.
22. *Sanhedrin* 4b.
23. See Maharatz Chajes, *Mavo HaTalmud*, Ch. 1.
24. **Berachot* 21b.
25. **Bava Kama* 82a.
26. *Shabbat* 82b.

argued that where the law concerned is of Sinaitic origin, the purpose of *drash* was to show that the oral tradition is contained in the Written Law.[27]

It has also been suggested that at a time when it was not permitted to commit the Oral Law to writing, *drash* served as a mnemonic to facilitate the process of memorizing.[28] Where the law concerned is of Rabbinic origin, it has been said that although the *drash* did not directly produce the law, it served as an indication to the Sages that an enactment of the law concerned is appropriate.[29(ז)]

Controversy between Malbim and R. Halevy

There is, of course, a type of *drash* which actually produced laws – that is, a *drash* which arose where a point of law was in question and the Sages turned to the Scripture in order to procure an answer by means of *drash*.

---

27. *Ohr HaChayim, Vayikra* 13:34; *Ritva, *Rosh Hashanah* 16a. *Shnei Luchot HaBrit* (*Shlah*) suggests in *Masechet Shevuot* that the purpose of *asmachta* was to allow that "there is nothing which the Sages have said that is not indicated in the Torah." (See *Hagah B'inyan Remez.*) See also Rambam, *Moreh Nevuchim*: "They use the text of the Bible as a kind of poetic language, and do not intend thereby to give an interpretation of the text."
28. "They connected the mitzvah to the Scripture as a sign that it be known and remembered" (Rambam, *Introduction to Seder Zeraim*); "or they used the verse as an *asmachta* or a sign for the tradition they had received...they connected them to a verse as an aid to memory" (R. Yehudah haLevi, *Kuzari, Maamar* 3, par. 73). See also *Tosafot, Menachot* 92b, s.v. "*Girse.*" If the latter purpose was intended, we think that this will explain why some *drash* was considered acceptable, although it appears to be far removed from the plain meaning of the Scripture; if its purpose was to serve as an aid to memory, then the most extraordinary *drash* would be the most effective. Joshua Heller (*Maoz HaDat* [Jerusalem, 1965], p. 12) argues that *drash* can be treated as a mnemonic only in cases where the law is of Rabbinic origin.(ח)
29. Ritva, *Rosh Hashanah* 16a. Also *Maharal of Prague, *Gur Aryeh, Parashat Yitro.* See R' S.B. Sofer, *Divrei Sofrim*, p. 8, that this argument is confined to laws of Rabbinic origin. A completely different purpose for *asmachta* is that suggested by Maharal (*Likutim*) namely that laws of Rabbinic origin were connected to the Bible to invest them with greater authority. A somewhat different argument is put forward by the *Shlah*(ט) who suggests that *asmachta* indicates that the idea underlying the relevant passage in the Biblical text on which the *asmachta* is based caused the Sages to enact the relevant law. (See *Torah sheBe'al Peh, klal Rabanan*). See also Rashi, *Berachot* 20b, s.v. "*Kideashkechan*," which it is suggested contains the same idea.

In fact, Malbim, a nineteenth-century Bible commentator, suggests[30] that most of the *drash* in the Talmud is of this type. He explains that the Sages in their *drash* followed special rules of language which were known to them. These rules of language have been long forgotten, and Malbim claims to have re-discovered them.[31]

R' I.I. Halevy, the Talmudist and historian, is of a different opinion.[32] He considers that *drash* of this type was very rare, and that in any event there were no such rules of language as Malbim suggests. Mostly, when a point of law was in doubt the Sages did not use creative *drash* at all. Generally, *drash* was used only after the Sages had already decided the law, having based their decision on tradition and logic.[33]

---

30. **Ayelet HaShachar,* Introduction to *Vayikra.*
31. Malbim lays down 613 rules which he claims were received by the *Tanna'im* for the purpose of interpreting the Hebrew language. The following is an example of one such rule, chosen at random. Rule 166 says: If there are two subjects to a verb, it must be in the plural, unless one of the subjects is the more active or the more important. He then goes on to examine the following text in the light of this rule: "This is the offering of Aharon and his sons which they shall sacrifice (*yakrivu*) to God" (*Vayikra* 6:13). This verse has two subjects "Aharon" and "his sons," and a verb in the plural *"yakrivu"* According to the rule stated, this means that neither one of the subjects is more active or important than the other. Now we can see that the following *drash* which appears in the *Sifra* flows from our rule. The *Sifra* says: "I would have thought that Aharon and his sons bring jointly *one* sacrifice. But the Scripture says 'his sons... sacrifice' (*yakrivu*). How can this be done? Aharon brings his own offering and his sons bring their own." In other words, the equality indicated by the verb in plural is achieved by each bringing separate offerings. Had a joint offering been brought, Aharon, as the High Priest, would have taken the major part in the proceeding.
32. **Dorot HaRishonim* 1:5, p. 487 et seq. See also Maharal of Prague, *Gur Aryeh, Parashat Yitro.*
33. To the question "Why does the Talmud so fiercely debate the validity of a particular Scriptural proof if, in fact, the Scriptural proof is only an *asmachta*?" R' Halevy provides no satisfactory answer. However, he points to the examples of laws of Rabbinic origin which are treated in the Talmud as derived by *drash.* In these cases, the *drash* is clearly no more than *asmachta,* yet the validity of the *drash* is frequently contested and fiercely argued.

SECTION III: THE OBLIGATION TO OBSERVE LAWS DERIVED BY MEANS OF *DRASH* AND *SVARA*

The obligation to observe the laws of the Torah in general arises out of a covenant between God and Israel: "And the Lord said to Moshe, 'Write for yourself these words; for after the tenor of these words I have made a covenant with you and with Israel.'"[34] The Talmud states that at first the Israelites entered into this covenant under coercion, but eventually ratified it voluntarily after the great wonder which they witnessed in the days of Achashverosh.[35]

Scriptural Authority for Rabbinic Interpretation

This covenant relates to the Torah which the Israelites received at Sinai and, consequently, also to the interpretation of the Torah by the Sages, since the Torah clothes this interpretation with authority:[36] "If there be any matter too hard for you in judgment.... You shall come to the Priest, the Levite, and to the judge that shall be in those days, and inquire...you shall observe to do according to all that they inform you."[37]

The duty to observe the laws derived by means of *drash* and *svara* is, accordingly, based upon the Torah (or *d'Oraita*)[38] in contradistinction to the duty to observe laws newly created by the Sages, which have a lower status (of *d'Rabanan*) and which, generally speaking, may be treated more leniently.[39]

34. *Shemot* 34:27.
35. *Shabbat* 88a.
36. See *Sefer HaMitzvot, Shoresh* 2, comment of Ramban. However, it must be noted that laws based on *drash* are in some respects treated less severely than laws expressly stated in the Torah. See also *Tosafot, Yevamot* 7b, s.v. *"V'omar"* Ran, *Nedarim* 8a; *Tosefot Yom-Tov,* Mishnah *Zevachim* 10:2.
37. *Devarim* 17:8-10.
38. See R' I.I. Halevy, op. cit. 1:5, p. 525, who states that while these interpretations are *d'Oraita,* they are liable to be reversed by a later *Bet Din* which considers the logic or *drash* to have been mistaken. See also *Gur Aryeh, Parashat Yitro.*
39. Sometimes the Sages ruled that their laws must be treated as severely, or even more severely, than Torah laws. See *Gittin* 65a, *Eruvin* 77a, and Mishnah *Ketubot* 4:1.

D'Oraita and d'Rabanan Distinguished

This distinction is emphasized most clearly in a case where a person is in doubt whether he has already discharged his obligation regarding a mitzvah. If the obligation is *d'Oraita,* he must take the stricter view; if it is *d'Rabanan,* he may take the more lenient one. For example, if a question arises whether the *tefillin* one has donned are kosher or whether one has already recited the Grace after Meals, a doubt has been raised concerning *d'Oraita* laws, and consequently the stricter view must be taken. A different pair of halachically kosher *tefillin* must be put on; or Grace after Meals has to be recited, although this may already have been done. However, when the doubt is whether one's hands were properly washed (*netilat yadayim*) before eating bread, one need not wash his hands again because the obligation is *d'Rabanan.*[40]

D'Oraita Status of Interpretative Laws

There is definite Talmudic authority for the proposition that laws derived by *svara* have *d'Oraita* status. On occasions, when in the Talmud one of the Sages quotes from the Bible to support a certain law, he is met with the objection, "Why quote from the Bible – it is *svara*!"[41] These statements show clearly that in the Talmud's view, logic carries the same weight as the Bible itself.

No such clear Talmudic authority can be found for laws derived by *drash.*[42] The most that can be said is that generally such laws are treated

40. *Berachot* 21a. Rabbinic laws are also treated more leniently in the following cases or circumstances:
    a. *Pesachim* 4b. A woman's evidence is admissible concerning a Rabbinic prohibition even in a case where she has an "interest" (e.g. to save herself trouble).
    b. *Ketubot* 28a. Where a Rabbinic law is concerned, evidence by a witness as to what he saw while he was still a minor, is admissible.
    c. *Shevuot* 23b. An oath not to comply with a Rabbinic decree is valid.
41. *Bava Kama* 46b.
42. Although there is no clear Talmudic authority for the proposition that such laws have *d'Oraita* status, there is a hint of this in *Pesachim* 18b: In connection with the *drash "Kal vaChomer"* (*de minore ad majus*) the Talmud states "although the law could have been deduced by *Kal vaChomer*, yet the Biblical text states it expressly."

by the authorities as of equal status with *d'Oraita* laws. For example, a woman who was "acquired" (in marriage) by "money" is treated as having *d'Oraita* marital status, even though the law that a "woman may be acquired by money" is derived by *drash*.[43] (*)

In this connection, however, reference has to be made to a famous dispute between Rambam and the twelfth-century Gerona Talmudist and exegete, Ramban. Rambam appears to be taking up a position contrary to what has been stated, namely, to be saying that laws derived by *drash* normally have no higher status than Rabbinic Law.[44]

Controversy between Rambam and Ramban

In his *Sefer HaMitzvot* Rambam enumerates the mitzvot of the Torah. According to a view expressed in the Talmud,[45] the number of such mitzvot is 613.[46] In order to arrive at this traditional number, Rambam excludes several of the enactments of the Torah. For example, he excludes mitzvot which applied only during a limited period of time,[47] and also mitzvot which are of a general nature and which do not require specific action to be taken.[48] He also excludes mitzvot which are derived by *drash*

[This shows that the Talmud equates a *Kal vaChomer* with an express Biblical statement, i.e. they are of equal status.] See *Nazir* 47b, *Kiddushin* 4b, and *Zevachim* 49b (in connection with *Mah Matzinu*); see also *Berachot* 20b, where a law deduced by *Hekesh* is called "from the Torah."

Although interpretive laws have *d'Oraita* status, they can be changed by a later *Bet Din* which is "greater in wisdom and numbers"; see Rambam, *Hilchot Mamrim* 2:1.

See also Nachum Rabinovitch, *Iyunim BeMishnato shel HaRambam* (Jerusalem, 1998), Chs. 3 and 4.

43. Mishnah *Kiddushin* 1:1 and *Kiddushin* 3b.
44. **Shoresh* 2.
45. *Makkot* 23.
46. See Introduction to *Kiryat Sefer* (Mabit) for the legal consequences which flow from the fact that a law is *d'Oraita* and (i) of the Oral Law but not of the Written Law, or (ii) of the Written Law, but not counted as one of the 613 mitzvot.
47. For instance, the prohibition against leaving Manna from one morning to the next (see *Shemot* 16:19), which applied only during the time when the Israelites sojourned in the desert.
48. For instance, the commandment: "In all that I have said to you, take heed" (*Shemot* 23:13).

and, in this connection, he makes the statement that such mitzvot must be presumed to be *d'Rabanan* where the contrary is not stated.[(כ)]

However, this last statement cannot be accepted as final since it is severely criticized by Ramban,[49] who states that such laws must be presumed to be *d'Oraita* in the absence of contrary evidence. Moreover, various commentators point out that Rambam classified a number of laws derived by *drash* as being *d'Oraita.*

The suggestion has been made that the original Arabic text of *Sefer HaMitzvot* has been mistranslated – that Rambam had not said that such laws have *d'Rabanan* status, but that laws derived by *drash* are *divrei sofrim*. In the terminology of Rambam, the expression "*divrei sofrim*" includes all laws which are not expressly stated in the Scripture,[50] whether they have *d'Oraita* status or not. In that view, Rambam would agree that laws derived by *drash* which are *divrei sofrim* have *d'Oraita* status in every respect.[51]

The Status of Rabbinic Laws Varies According to Whether the Sages Were Legislating or Interpreting

If laws derived by means of *drash* and logic have the status of *d'Oraita,* notwithstanding that they are not of Sinaitic origin, why have *Gezerot* and *Takkanot* the inferior status of *d'Rabanan*? The answer appears to be that whereas the Sages have a function in producing both types of law, their function is different in each case. The Sages produced laws derived by *drash* and logic as *interpreters* of Sinaitic Law. They produced *Gezerot* and *Takkanot* as *legislators*. For example, when the Sages stated that it is

49. *Ad loc.

50. *Kinat Sofrim,* ad loc. See Rambam's definition of *divrei sofrim* in Mishnah *Kelim* 17:12 and Mishnah *Mikva'ot* 7:7.

51. **Megillat Esther,* ad loc. He also suggests that Rambam is not at all concerned in distinguishing between *d'Oraita* and *d'Rabanan,* but between laws which can be *counted* among the 613 and those which cannot. *Lev Same'ach* suggests that Rambam accords *d'Oraita* status to laws derived by *drash* only where the *drash* concerns a detail of a law which is in itself *d'Oraita,* e.g. the principle of *Kiddushin* is *d'Oraita,* therefore the *drash* enabling *Kiddushin* by "money" is also *d'Oraita.*

See also *Tashbatz* 1:1:151 and R' I.I. Halevy, *Dorot HaRishomim* 1:5, pp. 514–542.

prohibited to kill an innocent man even in order to save one's own life,[52] they were interpreting the Sinaitic law "You shall not kill."[53] Similarly, in other cases they were interpreting the intention of the Torah in a general sense, even if they were not interpreting a specific Scriptural law. In laws based on logic they were in fact saying, "This law is so obvious that the Torah must have intended it."[ל]

On the other hand, when the Sages stated the law of *Muktzeh*[54] they were *creating* a new law; they had the tradition that only thirty-nine types of "work" were prohibited on the Sabbath,[55] and therefore "You shall do no work"[56] could not be interpreted to include the prohibition of *Muktzeh.* This is an instance of new law being made by the Sages. Wherever the Sages acted as *interpreters* they did not actually *make* the law and the law is therefore *d'Oraita;* wherever they acted as legislators they *made* the law and the law is, accordingly, *d'Rabanan.*[57]

52. See *Sanhedrin* 74a.
53. *Shemot* 20:13.
54. This law prohibits the handling of objects on the Sabbath which one would not expect to use that day: e.g. because the object only came into being on the Sabbath; or because it is repulsive; or because it is altogether too valuable for use; or because it serves a purpose which is inappropriate for the Sabbath, e.g. to make fire.
55. *Shabbat* 73a.
56. *Shemot* 20:10.
57. For the distinction between interpretive laws and others, see also *Sermons of the Ran* (Sermon 7), and Prof. M. Elon, *Israel Law Review,* Vol. 9, no. 4, p. 542 et seq.

Notes of Rav Simcha Wasserman זצ״ל

א. הכתוב מסרו לחכמים.

ב. לא שייך להנ״ל אלא הוא כעין סברא די״ג מדות. [נראה בכוונתו דזו סוג סברא אחרת מהיכא שהתורה מסרה לחכמים להחליט את הדין ברוחב בינתם כפי שמסתבר להם דבכאן עליהם למצא סברת התורה ולפרש כוונתה על פי המדות שהתורה נדרשת בהן.]

ג. כוונתם ב״מה לי אפוקי ומה לי עיולי״ הוא לומר דהיינו הך, וזה יותר חזק מסברא שהוא כעין דרוש.

[הערת העורך: כנים הדברים לרמב״ן בשבת דף ג. שכתב אליבא דר׳ פפא דגם הכנסה אב הוא כמו הוצאה. וכן משמע ברמב״ם פי״ב משבת ה״ח. אבל להסוברים דאינו אלא תולדה לכאורה אינו אלא כמו דרשה.]

ד. האם מיגו משום ראיה? [ע׳ בזה קובץ שיעורים ח״ב סי׳ ג׳ שחידש דהוא משום כח הטענה] וכל זה טעון עיון מיוחד בממון באיזה ראיה סגי.

ה. גם הסברא היא מי״ג מדות כמו ק״ו ובנין אב. [כוונת ההערה דק״ו ובנין אב הם מדות הבנויים על אדני ההגיון, וסברא היא ענף מהן כלשון הרש״ו במכתבו למחה״ס, ולכן אין לומר דכשהוציאו הדין בי״ג מדות לא השתמשו בסברא.]

ו. לא שייך לי״ג מדות, וזו עוד כוונה נוספת בכתוב.

ז. היינו שזה רצון ה׳, והאריך בזה רא״ב וסרמן ז״ל בקונטרס דברי סופרים סימן א׳ אות י״ז עד כ״ד.

ח. תוס׳ סוכה טבלא המתהפכת סוכה ה׳ ע״א ד״ה מסגרתו. [ע״ש בתוס׳ שכתבו

״ומבעיא לן אי דרשה גמורה או אסמכתא בעלמא״, ומשמע דעל הצד שהוא דין תורה בהכרח הוא דרשה גמורה ולא אסמכתא בעלמא.]

ט. זהו ג״כ רצון ה׳ [ולמה הפריד מחה״ס בין דברי הריטב״א ומהר״ל לבין דברי השל״ה].

י. לא שאין הדרש ברור אלא שאין יכולין לפסוק על ידו כמו רמז. אני מביא לכם ראיה מן התורה וכו׳ (נדה ל׳ ע״ב), נחש לכמה מוליד וכו׳ (בכורות ח׳ ע״א). [לשון הגמ׳ שם ע״א הוא: נחש לשבע שנים וכו׳ מנה״מ וכו׳ שנא׳ ארור אתה מכל הבהמה וכו׳ אלא לומר לך א׳ לשבעה.]

[הערת העורך: מסופקני אם ירדתי לעומק הכוונה. מחה״ס רומז לכך שקיימת חולשה בדרש לעומת סברא כדמוכח מזה שסברא בודאי דאורייתא ובדרגת הכתוב בתורה ממש ואילו דרש הוא לכל היותר שוה בדין לדאורייתא. וע״ז העיר הרש״ו שאין זה מחמת שאין הדרש ברור דמצינו מקומות שהדרש ברור ועכ״ז לא ע״ז סמכו למעשה כיון שאינה מי״ג מדות ורק על ההלכה המקובלת, ולא הובא הדרש אלא כרמז בעלמא. ולפ״ז אולי נתכוין הרש״ו בזה דכש״כ שאין לייחס חולשה לאותן דרשות די״ג מדות שמהם למדו הלכה למעשה וצ״ע.]

כ. עיי״ש במגילת אסתר בשם בעל זוהר הרקיע [שביאר דדבר הנלמד מי״ג מדות לא קראם הרמב״ם דרבנן אלא מפני שהם פירשוהו לנו ולא בא בפירוש בתורה] ושם כ״ה ע״א כ׳ הרמב״ם ומה שראוי יותר למנותו והוא הנלמד בי״ג מדות וכו׳ מבואר די״ג מדות עדיף מאות יתירא [כגון כבד ״את״ אביך לרבות אחיך הגדול, הרי דלא תליא במה שהוא מפורש בתורה. אכן ילה״ע דגם שם לא היינו יודעים כוונת הרבוי אילולי רבנן.]

ל. סברא היא אחת מי״ג מדות כגון ק״ו ובנין אב. [וכמבואר לעיל הערה ז.]

Hebrew Sources

SECTION I

Questions of Law Specifically Delegated to the Sages

3. Chagigah 18a

תניא אידך: ״ששת ימים תאכל מצות וביום השביעי עצרת לה׳״ מה שביעי עצור אף ששת ימים עצורין. אי מה שביעי עצור בכל מלאכה אף ששת ימים עצורין בכל מלאכה תלמוד לומר ״וביום השביעי עצרת״ השביעי עצור בכל מלאכה ואין ששה ימים עצורין בכל מלאכה. הא לא מסרן הכתוב אלא לחכמים לומר לך אי זה יום אסור ואי זה יום מותר אי זו מלאכה אסורה ואי זו מלאכה מותרת.

3. Shnei Luchot HaBrit, Torah sheBe'al Peh, klal Rabanan

ד׳ עניינים הם מישך שייכי בדרבנן: א. היא דרבנן והיא מדאורייתא שהתורה נתנה ביד החכמים כמ״ש מקצת הפוסקים בענין מלאכת חול המועד שהוא מדאורייתא אלא שהתורה מסרה לחכמים שיאסרו המלאכות שנראה להם ויתירו מה שנראה להם.

4. Kreti, Yoreh De'ah, Trefut 29 1:5

שמונה מיני טריפות הן. דרוסה נקובה וכו׳: בגמרא נאמר הלכה למשה מסיני הם... שנמסרו כך דרך כלל טריפות נקובה וכו׳ וחז״ל כפי חכמתם ועוצם בינתם בפלפל התורה וכדומה ברוו ענין כלל הוא איך יסתעף הימנה פרטיה.

5. R. Nissim (Ran), Mishnah Yoma 1:1

ובגמרא נמי אמרנן דמי שיש לו חטטים בראשו סך כדרכו ואינו חושש ומי שידיו מלוכלכות בטיט ובצואה רוחץ כדרכו ואינו חושש ואי סיכה ורחיצה דאורייתא נינהו היכי מקילינן בהו הכי אלא ודאי מדרבנן נינהו והיינו נמי דאמרינן בגמ׳ ״הני חמישה ענויין כנגד מי?״ ומדאמרינן כנגד מי ולא אמרינן מנא לן משמע דמדרבנן נינהו ולא בעי אלא אם יש להם שום רמז מן התורה - ענוש כרת אלא על האוכל

ועל השותה ועושה מלאכה בלבד, ואם איתא דהני ענויי אחריני מדרבנן בעלמא נינהו יהיה שייך למימר בהו ״ולא אמרו ענוש כרת״ דהא אפי׳ איסורא דאורייתא נמי ליכא. לפיכך היה נראה לי דכולהו מדאורייתא נינהו אלא דכיון דלאו בכלל ענויי דכתיבי בקרא בהדיא באורייתא נינהו אלא מריבויא דשבתון אתו וכדאיתא בגמרא קילי טפי ומסרן הכתוב לחכמים והן הקלו בהן כפי מה שראו והתירו כל שאינו נעשה לתענוג.

Laws Deduced by Logic

6. Shabbat 96b

אשכחן הוצאה, הכנסה מנלן סברא היא מרשות לרשות הוא מה לי אפוקי ומה לי עיולי.

SECTION II

Drash Where the Law is of Sinaitic Origin

14. Rambam, Introduction to Seder Zeraim

שהפרושים המקבלים מפי משה - אין מחלקת בהם בשום פנים.

שהרי מאז ועד עתה לא מצאנו מחלקת שנפלה בזמן מן הזמנים... במה שאמר הכתוב ״פרי עץ הדר״ כדי שיאמר אחד שהוא אתרוג, ויאמר אחר שהוא חבושים או רמונים... וכיוצא בהן בכלל המצוות אין מחלוקת בהן שכולן פרושים מקובלים מפי משה, ועליהם ועל דומיהם אמרו ״כל התורה נאמרו כללותיה ופרטותיה ודקדוקיה מסיני״ אבל אף על פי שהם מקובלים ואין מחלוקת בהם - הרי היא מחכמת התורה הנתונה לנו, שנוכל להוציא ממנה אלו הפירושים בדרך מדרכי הסברות, והאסמכתות והראיות והרמזים המצויים במקרא - וכשתראה אותם בתלמוד מעיינים וחולקים זה על זה במערכת העיון ומביאין ראיות על אחד מאלו הפרושים והדומה להם, כגון מה שאמרו במאמר ״פרי עץ הדר״ אולי יהיה רמונים או חבושים או זולתם עד שהביאו ראיה עליו ממה שנאמר ״פרי עץ הדר״ ואמרו ״עץ שטעם עצו ופריו שוין״ ואמר אחר ״פרי הדר באילנות משנה לשנה״ ואמר אחר ״פרי הדר על כל מים״ - אלו הראיות לא הביאון מפני שנשתבש עליהם הענין עד שנודע להם מהראיות האלה; אבל ראינו בלא ספק מיהושע עד עתה שהאתרוג היו לוקחים עם הלולב בכל שנה ואין בו מחלוקת אבל חקרו על הרמז הנמצא בכתוב לזה הפרוש המקובל.

14. Ohr HaChayim, Vayikra 13:34

וראיתי ליישב מאמרי ז״ל שאמרו שלא היה דבר שלא נמסר למשה בסיני ואפילו מה שתלמיד ותיק עתיד לחדש. ואמרו במקום אחר כי רבי עקיבא הי׳ דורש מה שלא ידע משה. כאומר הדברים עשיתים אעשה לא נאמר וכו׳ יעש״ד. וכן כמה מאמרים שדומים לזה. ונראה כי ישוב המאמרים הוא כי הן אמת שכל דבר תורה נאמ׳ למשה ואין חכם יכול לדעת יותר ממה שידע משה. והגם שתצרף כל דורות ישראל מיום מתן תורה עד שתמלא הארץ דעה אין חידוש שלא ידע משה. אבל ההפרש הוא כי משה נתן לו ה׳ תורה שבכתב ותורה שבעל פה. והנ׳ האדון ב״ה בחכמתו ית׳ רשם בתורה שבכתב כל התורה שבעל פה שאמר למשה אבל לא הודיע למשה כל מה שנתן לו בע״פ היכן רמוז בתורה שבכתב. וזו היא עבודת בני ישראל עמלי תורה שיישבו ההלכות שנאמרו למשה בסיני והסודות והדרשות כלן יתנו להם מקום בתורה שבכתב. ולזה תמצא באומ׳ התנאים וחברו ת״כ וספרי וכו׳ וכל דרשותם בכתובים אינם אלא ע״פ ההלכות. והלבישו׳ בתורת ה׳ תמימה שבכתב ואחריה׳. ועד היום זו היא עבודת הקודש בני תורה לדייק המקראות וליישב ע״פ המאמרים שהם תורה שבעל פה. וזו היא עבוד׳ התורה הנקראת ארץ החיים. וענין זה לא נמסר למשה כולו לדעת כל תורה שבעל פה היכן היא כולה רמוזה בתורה שבכתב. ולזה אמרו ז״ל שדרש ר״ע דרשות שלא ידעם משה, אין הכוונה שלא ידע משה עקרן של דברים, הלא ממנו הכל אפי׳ מה שתלמיד ותיק עתיד לחדש. אלא שלא ידע סמיכתם ודיוקם היכן רמוזים בתורה. וזה לך האות מה שלפנינו, שדרש הלל מהכתוב ההלכה שנאמרה למשה בעל פה ולא גילה ה׳ למשה עקרה בכתוב, ובא הלל ודרשה. ודברים אלו נכונים הם.

Drash Where the Law is Based on Logic

15. Sanhedrin 78a

תנו רבנן הכוהו עשרה בני אדם בעשרה מקלות ומת בין בבת אחת בין בזה אחר זה פטורין. ר׳ יהודה בן בתירא אומר בזה אחר זה האחרון חייב מפני שקירב את מיתתו. אמר ר׳ יוחנן ושניהם מקרא אחד דרשו ״ואיש כי יכה כל נפש אדם״ רבנן סברי כל נפש וכו׳... ור׳ יהודה בן בתירא סבר כל נפש וכו׳... אמר רבא הכל מודים בהורג את הטריפה שהוא פטור בגוסס בידי שמים שהוא חייב לא נחלקו אלא בגוסס בידי אדם מר מדמי ליה לטרפה ומר מדמי ליה לגוסס.

Drash Where the Law is of Rabbinic Origin

24. Berachot 21b

מנין לבעל קרי שאסור בדברי תורה שנאמר ״והודעתם לבניך לבני בניך״ וסמיך

ליה "יום אשר עמדת וגו'" מה להלן בעלי קריין אסורין אף כאן בעלי קריין אסורין וכי תימא ר"י לא דריש סמוכים וכו'.

25. Bava Kama 82a

עשרה תקנות תיקן עזרא... ותיקן טבילה לבעלי קריין.

Scripture Indicates That an Enactment of a Law by the Sages Is Appropriate

27. Ritva, Rosh Hashanah 16a

שכל מה שיש לו אסמכתא מן הפסוק העיר הקב"ה שראוי לעשות כן אלא שלא קבעו חובה ומסרו לחכמים. וזה דבר ברור ואמת ולא כדברי המפרשים האסמכתאות שהוא כדרך סמן שנתנו חכמים ואל שכונת התורה לכך ח"ו ישתקע הדבר ולא יאמר שזו דעת מינות הוא אבל התורה העירה בכך ומסרו חיוב הדבר לקבעו חכמים אם ירצו כמ"ש ועשית ע"פ הדבר אשר יגידו לך ולפיכך תמצא החכמים נותנים בכל מקום ראיה או זכר או אסמכתא לדבריהם מן התורה כלומר שאינם מחדשים דבר מלבם וכל תורה שבע"פ רמוזה בתורה שהיא תמימה וח"ו שהיא חסירה כלום.

29. Maharal of Prague, Gur Aryeh, Parashat Yitro

ואל תטעה לומר, כי בכל מקום שאמרו ז"ל אסמכתא היא, שמשה רבנו כאשר כתב התורה לא כתב אותו בשביל אותה אסמכתא, רק הם ז"ל אסמכוה אותה מדעתם. אומר אני, האומר כן טועה בדברי חכמים שאם כן יהיו דברי חכמים רק עמל ויגיעה ואין בו ממש, שלפעמים מוציאים דבר מן המקרא על ידי לימוד דרשות ולא יהיה זה רק ליפות הדברים או לגנוב דעת הבריות כאילו היא דרשה מן התורה, ולא נאה זה לחכם, שהרי אין להם שום חלק ונחלה בתורה אלא הם ז"ל אסמוכה אותה מדעתם אקרא. אבל כך פירושו שיש לדבריהם אסמכתא - שדבריהם נסמכים אקרא, ונקרא זה אסמכתא, כלומר שאין זה גוף המקרא אלא שנסמכים דבריהם על דברי תורה ומחוברים אל דברי התורה, ולעולם בתורה יש להם חלק. לפעמים הוא פירוש הכתוב, כמו גבי תפילין שעיקרו מדברי תורה ופירושו מדברי סופרים, ואין זה אסמכתא אלא פירוש דברי תורה, וכן הרבה למאד. כי מאחר שהדרשה בעצמה חכמים דרשוה נקרא זה דברי סופרים כל דבר הבא מדעתם ושכלם, וזה הדבר יש לו דין דברי תורה, אבל לפעמים אין הגוף דברי תורה רק נסמך לדברי תורה ומצטרף על דברי תורה, וכיון דלא הוי רק שנסמך על דברי תורה יש לו דין אחר, דהוי מדרבנן לגמרי. כי נראה לי כל הדרשות שדרשו חכמים כולן הן

מן התורה, ולא שהן גוף התורה רק הן יוצאות מן התורה. דמיון זה הבנאי בונה בית והניח מקום להעמיד שם דברים הצריכים אל הבית, ובא אחר כך חכם אחד ומתבונן בבית, למה בנה הבית בצורה זאת - רק להוסיף דבר זה, ועוד בנאו בצורה זאת להוסיף דבר זה. הנה כל התוספות הוסיף האיש החכם, אבל הוא לקח אותם מבנין הבית, ולפעמים החכם מבאר ומפרש איזה דבר נקרא בית ואיזה חדר, ואין זה תוספות רק פירוש וביאור. כך התורה ניתנה בלא תוספות בלא מגרעת, והניחה לחכמים מקום, והם הרמזים בתורה ומכל מקום מאחר שלא כתב זאת בפירוש כאילו אמרה תורה: אתם החכמים יש לכם במקום הזה להוסיף והיא דעתכם. אבל אין כל כך דבר הכרחי כמו דעת בתורה, שזה החילוק בין הדברים שהם אסמכתא, שאין כל כך הכרחי כמו דברי תורה. אך עתה עמדו דרשנים דורשים דברים אשר לא כן כל העולה על רוחם ודעתם, ואין ספק אלי שהתורה חוגרת שק עליהם, לפרש התורה כרצונם. וזהו מעשה האומות שמפרשים כרצונם ובזה האמת נעדרת תחת אשר נקראת תורת אמת.

The Sages Followed Special Rules of Language Which Were Known to Them

30. Malbim, Ayelet HaShachar, Introduction to Vayikra

על זאת נשמו אחרונים וקדמונים התפלאו, לאמר זאת התורה אשר לנו הנקראת בשם תורה שבע"פ מה יסודה...

כי כל מעיין...יראה שהיא נסמכת תמיד על משענת הכתובים ונדרשת מן המקראות...אולם כאשר נבקר את הכתובים עצמם...נראה שלא לבד שאין פשט המקרא מכריח את הדרוש ההוא שהוציאו ממנו כי גם לפעמים היה בהפך...

וכאשר שאלנו לדור ראשון ומזקנים נתבונן מה ענו על זאת, ראינו כי מלבם יוציאו מלים שהכתובים המובאים לראיה אל ההלכות הם רק ציונים ואסמכתות אשר הציבו להם ציונים לעורר הזכרון. ועקרי ההלכות היו מקובלות בידם בעל פה וזה רחוק מאד...חיבורי הנוכחי...הוא ילחם את אויבי הקבלה בשער... ובא בו האות והמופת כי תורת הפה היא התורה שנתנה מן השמים וכי כל דברי תורה שבע"פ מוכרחים ומוטבעים בפשט הכתוב ובעומק הלשון. וכי הדרוש הוא לבדו הוא הפשט הפשוט המיוסד כפי חוקי הלשון האמיתיים והברורים. וכל מקום אשר דרשו חז"ל איזה דרוש יש שם איזה זר היוצא מכללי הלשון. וע"י הדרוש ישוב הכתוב לאיתנו כמשפט הלשון וחוקותיו. וכל דרש אשר דרשו אינו בודד במקום ההוא לבדו רק כן דרשו וכן פירשו בכ"מ אשר בא הזרות הזה.

The Sages Did Not Use "Creative" Drash at All

32. R' I.I. Halevy, Dorot HaRishonim 1:5, p. 487

והלא הדבר הזה לבדו די להכריע ולברר את כל הדבר כמו שהוא. שכל הדרשות בדרכי הדרשות השתמשו בהם רק או לסמוך את הקבלה הידועה והחלוטה בדרך של ליכא מידי דלא רמיזי בקרא, או גם לתמוך את דבריהם במקום שהחליטו והכריעו כן מתוך יסודי המשנה או מתוך קבלתם מרבותיהם או מתוך הסברא מתוך ידיעת יסודי התורה. אבל לא להכריע במקום שהיה להם ספק, וכשלא יכלו להכריע הדבר מתוך יסודי הקבלה או מסברה גמורה של דרכי התורה.

SECTION III

Laws Derived by Drash Normally Have d'Rabanan Status

44. Rambam, Sefer HaMitzvot, Shoresh 2

השרש השני שאין ראוי למנות כל מה שלמדים באחת משלש עשרה מדות שהתורה נדרשת בהן או מרבוי:

כבר בארנו בפתיחת חבורינו בפירוש המשנה שרוב דיני התורה יצאו בשלש עשרה מדות... הנה פעמים תפול בו המחלוקת ושיש שם דינין הן פירושים מקובלים ממשה אין מחלוקת בהם אבל הם מביאים ראיה עליהן באחת משלש עשרה מידות כי מחכמת הכתוב שהוא אפשר שיצא בו רמז מורה על הפירוש ההוא המקובל או היקש יורה עליו וכבר בארנו זה הענין שם. וכשיהיה זה כן הנה לא כל מה שנמצא לחכמים שהוציאו בהיקש משלש עשרה מדות נאמר שהוא נאמר למשה בסיני ולא גם כן נאמר בכל מה שימצא בתלמוד שיסמכוהו אל אחת משלש עשרה מדות שהוא דרבנן, כי פעמים יהיה הפירוש ההוא מקובל ממשה בסיני לפי הראוי בזה שכל מה שלא תמצאהו כתוב בתורה ותמצאהו בתלמוד שלמדוהו באחת משלש עשרה מדות אם בארו הם בעצמם ואמרו שזה גוף תורה או שזה דאורייתא הנה ראוי למנותו אחר שהמקובלים ממנו אמרו שהוא דאורייתא. ואם לא יבארו זה ולא דברו בו הנה הוא דרבנן שאין שם כתוב יורה עליו.

49. Ramban, ad loc.

...ולפי זה הראוי הוא שנאמר בהפך שכל דבר הנדרש בתלמוד באחת מכל י״ג מידות הוא מדאורייתא עד שנשמע אותם שיאמרו שהוא אסמכתא.

51. *Megillat Esther, ad loc.*

שגם זו היא כונת הרב שכל דבר הנלמד בי״ג המדות הוא מן התורה ודינו כדין הדברים המפורשים בתורה רק שלא יבואו במנין תרי״ג מצוות... כן הוא כל דבר הנלמד מהמדות אצל רז״ל דין תורה אף על פי שהוא קורא אותם מד״ס. וכן בפי׳ המשנה בפ׳ י״ז במסכת כלים הוא כתב כי מאמר ד״ס יכלול שיהא הדבר דעת סופרים כמו הפירושים וההלכות המקובלים ממשה והולכין בספק להחמיר.

Chapter 3

Halachah and Morality – the Moral *Svara*

INTRODUCTION

In the previous chapter we have seen that *svara,* meaning *logic,* was a tool of interpretation.

In this chapter we explain that *svara* also had another meaning – *moral reasoning,* and we discuss the contribution moral reasoning or moral *svara* made to Oral law.

We end the chapter by discussing halachic statements of the Sages which appear to contradict moral reasoning.

SECTION I: *SVARA* AS MORAL REASONING – AN EXAMPLE

Kill or be Killed

Rabbah's ruling that one must not kill an innocent man even in order to save one's own life is based on the moral *svara* "who told you that your blood is redder than his?"[1]

1. *Sanhedrin 74a.

The Talmud asks: "*rotze'ach gufa mina lon*" – from where do we know this law that one must allow oneself to be killed rather than kill? And the Talmud answers: "*Svara hi*"– it is based on *svara*. The Talmud then reports: A man came before Rabbah and said to him, "The governor of my town ordered me to kill X, and he added that if you do not kill X I will kill you". The man asked Rabbah what to do. Rabbah said to him "Let him kill you and do not kill X. Who says your blood is redder than that of X?"

This is clearly "moral reasoning" and not logic. One could argue: one life has to be lost, it is permissible to save one's own life rather than that of the other person.

Can Moral Reasoning Create New Mitzvot?

Moral reasoning interprets *halachah*. The case of "kill or be killed" interprets either "*lo tirtzach*" (the prohibition against murder) or "*vechai bahem*" (the principle that danger to life entitles one to ignore mitzvot). But can moral reasoning create a new mitzvah?

The Talmud suggests that the mitzvah which requires a blessing before eating food, etc., is a *svara*, namely that one is forbidden to enjoy the products of this world without thanking God.[2] Clearly a moral *svara*. Logically one could argue that God, who brought us to this world, has an obligation to feed us.

This *halachah* is an entirely new mitzvah and is created by a moral *svara*. However, it is generally considered to be Rabbinic *legislation*, and not *interpretation*, in which case we have no proof.

SECTION II: MORAL *SVARA* AND INTERPRETATION

It is instructive to contrast the wide interpretation of mitzvot which convey a positive moral message with the opposite approach of narrow interpretation in mitzvot which appear to contradict moral reasoning.

One example is the prohibition of "*lifnei iver lo titen michshol,*"[3]

2. **Berachot* 35a.
3. *Vayikra* 19:14.

not to place a stumbling block in front of a blind person. The simple understanding of the verse means no more than placing an obstacle in the path of a blind man. The Sages, however, expanded this prohibition to include the giving of bad advice,[4] helping others transgress commandments,[5] and even forbidding the hitting of an adult son in case he might retaliate and hit his father.[6]

Another example of this phenomenon includes the law forbidding the withholding of wages of a day worker after nightfall. The Torah writes: "Give him his pay that day; do not let the sun set on him, for he is poor..." (*Devarim* 24:14). Yet the Sages apply this law to all workers, rich and poor alike.

The instruction of fencing off a roof is presented as follows: "When you build a new house you shall make a fence for your roof" (*Devarim* 22:8). The Sages did not limit this commandment to building a new house, but included buying a house. Furthermore they understood it to refer as well to pits, caves, and underground constructions.[7] [8]

Moral Svara That Leads to Restrictive Interpretation

There is an important rule of interpretation. "*Ein lecha bo ela chiddusho*" – one cannot extend a stated *chiddush*.[9]

---

4. *Sifra* chapter 3 note 14, quoted by Rashi ibid. s.v. "*v'lifnei iver.*"
5. *Avodah Zara* 6b.
6. *Moed Katan* 17a, see Rashi there s.v. "*d'ka avar.*"
7. *Sifrei Devarim* section 229.
8. A further rule, "*derachehah darchei noam,*" is an example of restrictive interpretation of *hilchot yibbum*. The Sages, in their interpretation, were often guided by the rule "*derachehah darchei noam*" – the ways of the Torah are pleasant (*Mishlei* 3:17).

   The following is an illustration of how this principle was applied. The mitzvah of *yibbum* prescribes that if a man dies without children, his widow must marry his brother or perform *chalitzah*. What if at the time of death there was a child, but that child dies later? Does the woman then have to do *yibbum* or *chalitzah*? The Talmud says she does not, for the ways of the Torah are pleasant. A woman may have remarried in the interim, and it is morally repugnant to force her to undergo *chalitzah* with one man while married to another. Therefore, the Sages ruled that even a woman who has not remarried does not need *chalitzah* or *yibbum* in that particular case.
9. *Shevuot* 25b; *Temurah* 13b.

Ein Lecha Bo Ela Chiddusho

The term "*chiddush*" is described by Rashi as a *halachah* which does not conform to normal principles of the Torah.[10]

In a different context the *Noda B'yehuda*[11] writes that a *chiddush* is a command or principle which runs contrary to *svara*.

We will illustrate this further with the following examples.

Ben Sorer Umoreh

The law of *ben sorer umoreh* – a rebellious son (*Devarim* 21:18-21) – refers to a young boy who steals from his father in order to feast on meat and wine. If the boy was warned and punished by *Bet Din* and continues stealing, he is brought to *Bet Din* by his parents and put to death. Rabbi Yosei Haglili is quoted as wondering as to the justification for the death penalty that is prescribed to a *ben sorer umoreh*. He asks:

Because this boy ate a *tarteimer* of meat and drank half a *log* of Italian wine, the Torah declares that he must be taken out to be stoned?[12]

It is clear that that to kill a boy for a crime of theft and gluttony runs contrary to Torah principles of morality. The Sages therefore consider it to be a *chiddush*, and they interpreted its laws restrictively.

For instance, the Torah speaks about a rebellious son; the Sages did not extend the law to a rebellious daughter. Under normal circumstances one would expect the Sages to extend this law to girls as well. They did not. Because the law of *ben sorer umoreh* is a *chiddush*, it runs contrary to basic moral principles, and the Sages gave the narrowest interpretation possible.[13]

This is only one of many restrictive interpretations by the Sages

---

10. *Pesachim* 42b, s.v. "*chiddush.*"
11. Collection of responsa written by Rabbi Yechezkel Landau, an eighteenth-century Talmudist and Halachic authority. It should be noted that this particular resp. (Vol. II, *Yoreh De'ah* 36) was in fact written by his son, Rabbi Shmuel Landau.
12. *Sanhedrin* 71a.
13. *Sanhedrin* 68b. The understanding we have just presented is not explicit in the Talmud; it is based on *Lechem Mishneh*'s explanation of this law as he explains it in his commentary to Rambam, *Hilchot Mamrim* 7:11.

relating to *ben sorer umoreh*.[14] This makes the likelihood of all of the conditions of *ben sorer umoreh* being met so unlikely that the Sages declared: An instance of *ben sorer umoreh* has never occurred and never will.[15]

It is apparent that the Sages saw that this law does not conform to moral *svara*. And as a *chiddush* they limited its application to the utmost.[16]

Eidim Zomemim

Another example of *chiddush* is *eidim zomemim* – scheming witnesses (*Devarim* 19:16-19). *Eidim zomemim* are witnesses who, after testifying to a certain event, are challenged by a second group of witnesses who allege that these first witnesses could not have witnessed the act in question, as at the time of the given event they were with them elsewhere. The rule in such a case is that the second set of witnesses are believed. The first group of witnesses are presumed to have testified falsely, and they are now permanently disqualified from giving testimony in any legal dispute.

All principles of logic, and morality, tell us that both sets of witnesses must be treated the same. We either disqualify both groups or validate both of them for future testimonies. Consequently, the legitimacy of disqualifying only one set of witnesses is described as a *chiddush*. The Sages were therefore not prepared to apply this law to any other situation.

SECTION III: MORAL *SVARA* AND MITZVOT

Leniencies in Mitzvot Ben Adam Lechaveiro

HaGaon Rav Osher Weiss writes:

Regarding *mitzvot ben adam lechaveiro* there are many places in the Talmud and *Poskim* where they were lenient *without providing a clear*

14. Another example is the law that a *ben sorer umoreh* is only put to death if his father's voice and mother's voice are the same, because the Torah uses the word "*kolenu*" (our voice).
15. Ibid. 71a.
16. We would suggest that God did not expect the Sages to interpret *halachot* which were beyond human understanding. The approach must be: follow what is written and do not expand it.

halachic rationale for the leniency. It seems to me that the Sages, in their great wisdom understood that in situations where there is a need for the good of society and mankind, the Torah did not command these mitzvot.[17]

Rav Weiss gives an example of leniency in the case of *mitzvot ben adam lechaveiro*.

Rabbi Simlai's host was a *mamzer*, and Rabbi Simlai said to him, "Had I found out earlier I would have purified your sons." What was the advice that Rabbi Simlai would have given? He would have said to him, "Go and steal and be sold as a Hebrew slave."[18] [19]

In this case Rabbi Simlai was lenient with the prohibition of "*lo tignov*" and held it did not apply.[20]

We argue that in this particular case "moral *svara*" provides the clear halachic rationale which Rav Weiss seeks.[21]

Mitzvot ben adam lechaveiro are based on the great principle of *ve'ahavta lere'acha kamocha*. Let us establish what "*kamocha*" means.[22] It can be saying, "Everything you do for yourself you must also do for your

---

17. *Parashat Mishpatim* 5778 *Kovetz* 18.
18. *Kiddushin* 69a.
19. A Hebrew slave, even a *mamzer*, may marry a Canaanite maidservant. Any offspring of this union are slaves, and when freed, they become untainted Jews.
20. We have a problem, however, with Rav Weiss's explanation in the case of Rabbi Simlai. Rav Weiss argues the Torah never intended the prohibition of "*lo tignov*" to apply in this particular case. The problem is, if "*lo tignov*" does not apply, how can the *Bet Din* sell him? However, we would suggest that the words of Rav Yosef Engel in *Atvun d'Oraita* (chapter 9) answer that problem.

    According to Rav Engel, in *mitzvot ben adam lechaveiro*, although the prohibition of stealing is gone because of the extenuating circumstances, the debt remains. We will have to posit that *Bet Din* can sell a person because of a debt which came about by "stealing," even where the Torah says that in this particular case the prohibition of "*lo tignov*" does not apply.
21. Rav Weiss discusses many more cases, and what we say here may apply to some but not all of those cases.
22. We also have to establish what "*ve'ahavta*" means. Rav J. B. Soloveitchik writes "The plain conclusion is that with respect to love of one's fellow, it is the action that matters. When the action is performed, the commandment is fulfilled even though in its essence it involves a lofty cognitive emotional achievement. The ideal is reserved for the select few, but the means of realization are available to all" (*Halakhic Morality*, Maggid Books 2017, p.171).

fellow." Alternatively, it can be saying, "You do not have an obligation to do more for your fellow than what you would expect him to do for you."

Hillel considered that moral *svara* favored the latter interpretation. Hence he says "What you hate, do not do unto others."[23]

We now have our "clear halachic rationale." Would you – a reasonable and moral man – hate if someone who had no alternative way to remove the stigma of *mamzerut* would steal an easily replaceable object from you, and pay for it?

That, we suggest, is the moral *svara*, which provides a clear halachic rationale for the leniency in *mitzvot ben adam lechaveiro*, in this and in many similar cases.

Maybe this is what Rashba means when he wrote:[24] "Perhaps in these circumstances it is permitted, in order to purify his descendants."

SECTION IV: MORAL *SVARA* AND *HALACHOT* WHICH SEEM IMMORAL

We will now consider two halachic statements of the Sages which appear to contradict moral reasoning.[25]

Statement 1: The Sages say that a father can give his young daughter in marriage to a "*menuval v'mukke shechin*" – one who is disgusting and afflicted with boils.[26]

Statement 2: The Sages say that a master can say to his slave "*assei imi v'eini zancha*" – "you must work for me, but I will not provide you with any food."[27]

The reader may well ask: If the Sages interpreted *halachah* in accordance with moral reasoning, is it not unthinkable that a father be allowed such massive cruelty? The same can be asked about the master: How can it be moral to exploit a slave to such an extent?

---

23. *Shabbat* 31a.
24. Ad loc.; see also *Tosafot Rid.*
25. There are no doubt more than two problematic halachic statements to which the argument developed here is relevant.
26. *Ketubot* 40b.
27. *Gittin* 12a.

We suggest that one must distinguish between halachic rights and halachic power.

One cannot judge the morality of *halachah* by considering individual *halachot* on their own. There are four parts to *Shulchan Aruch,* and frequently in deciding practical *halachah* it is necessary to consider both *Choshen Mishpat* and *Even HaEzer,* and also *Orach Chayim* and *Yoreh De'ah.* The two above statements are *halachot* which belong to the category of civil law. Religious law provides the moral aspect and trumps civil law. This will become clear when we examine Statement 1 and Statement 2 in their context.

Statement 1: The Talmud discusses the question of who receives the payment of "*boshet*" and "*p'gam,*"[28] the father or the daughter? The Talmud concludes: "It is logical that the payment should belong to the father, *because he could give her in marriage to a menuval v'mukkeh shechin.*" It is clear that the Talmud here does not deal with the question of to whom the father is entitled to marry off his daughter (religious law). It deals with the question of who is entitled to the proceeds of a penalty (civil law).

Statement 2: The Talmud discusses whether it is a *zechut* (benefit) for the slave to attain his freedom or not. If the master is obliged to provide him with food, being freed would be construed as detrimental to the slave. It is here that the Talmud declares: "The master may say to his slave, 'Work for me and I will not provide you with any food.'" The issue discussed in the Talmud is not the duty or otherwise of the master to feed his slave (religious law). The issue is whether slavery is a *zechut* or a burden. This is a question which has civil law consequences.[29]

There are areas of Jewish jurisprudence where one has the power and authority to do a certain act, but is not allowed to exercise that power. In the case of Statement 1, if one were to ask, "Does a father *have the power* to marry his daughter to a *menuval v'mukkeh shechin*?" the answer is yes. However, if one were to ask, "*May* a father marry his daughter to

28. "*Boshet*" – shame, and "*p'gam*" – blemish, are penalties levied upon one who seduces or assaults a girl.

29. If it is a *zechut* any stranger can appoint himself as the slave's agent to receive the slave's *get shichrur* (freedom document).

a *menuval v'mukkeh shechin*?" the answer is no. In fact, the Talmud rules explicitly that it is forbidden to marry off a young girl until she is old enough to say, "I want to marry this man."[30]

In the case of Statement 2, if one were to ask, "Has a master the *power* to say to his slave, *'Assei imi v'eini zancha'*?" the answer is yes. However, if one were to ask, "*May* a master say to his slave slave, '*Assei imi ve'eini zancha*'?" the answer is no. In fact, Rambam writes: "A master may say to his Canaanite slave "*assei imi ve'eini zancha*." The slave may instead go and beg from door to door, and sustain himself that way, as Jews are commanded to sustain the slaves that are amongst them."[31] The master, apart from being a *master* is also a *Jew*. And clearly in common sense, the duty falls on him before it does on anybody else.[32] [33]

---

30. See *Kiddushin* 81b: אסור לאדם שיקדש את בתו כשהיא קטנה עד שתגדיל ותאמר בפלוני אני רוצה.
31. *Hilchot Avadim* 9:7. Rambam there continues:

> It is permitted to work a Canaanite slave harshly. Even though this is the law, a trait of piousness and the way of the wise is for a person to be merciful and to pursue righteousness, and not to overburden his slave and not to oppress him. He should feed him and give him to drink from all foods and drinks. The early Sages would give their slaves from every dish that they ate themselves, and would provide food for their animals and slaves before partaking of their own meals. Also, he should not embarrass him by his hand nor with words, for the Torah gave them to us to work, not to be humiliated. One should not shout or vent anger upon them excessively. Rather, one should speak with them patiently, and listen to their claims.

32. One may then well ask: If the father or master is entitled to such respective rights but must not exercise them, why give them the rights in the first place?

   We would suggest that the Sages considered Halachic jurisprudence as something created by God and true, just as the laws of physics where created by God and are true. This view is supported by the Sermons of the Ran (Sermon 11). Ran explains that *halachah* is entirely different to secular law. The latter is based on the convenience of society and to make social life as smooth as possible, whereas *halachah* is God's truth even though it may not be at all practical. He writes further that in the time of King David, though divine law ruled supreme, for practicality there was also *Mishpat haMelech*, the rule of the king. The fact that a father has the power to give his young daughter in marriage without restrictions, and that a master has no duty in civil law to feed his slave, is, we suggest, a divine truth. On a jurisprudential basis they were respectively the property of the father and the master. When times change and it is no longer appropriate to "own" slaves or young daughters – then God provided for his *Chachamim* to reinterpret or legislate as the situation demanded.
33. We do not think that we have explained all problems. There will always be laws in

Hebrew Sources

Laws Deduced by Svara

1. Sanhedrin 74a

רוצח גופיה מנא לן? סברא הוא דההוא דאתא לקמיה דרבה ואמר ליה אמר לי מרי דוראי (רש"י - אדון עירי ונכרי הוה) זיל קטליה לפלניא ואי לא קטלינא לך אמר ליה לקטלוך ולא תקטול - מי יימר לך דדמא דידך סומק טפי - דילמא דמא דהוא גברא סומק טפי.

2. Berachot 35a

כיצד מברכין על הפירות וכו'. מנא ה"מ? ...סברא הוא אסור לו לאדם שיהנה מן העולם הזה בלא ברכה.

---

the Torah which we cannot explain, and which we cannot understand. We think it appropriate to quote the words of the great rationalist, the Rambam, who writes:

> It is appropriate for any man to contemplate the laws of the Holy Torah and to understand their full depths according to his power to do so. Any mitzvah for which he cannot find a reason and does not know it purpose should not be taken lightly... His thoughts regarding the Torah should not be like his thoughts regarding secular matters. Come and see how stringent the Torah was with the law of *me'ilah* [unsanctioned use of sanctified objects]. If mere wood, stones, and dirt – once they have had the name of God pronounced on them – become sanctified, and one who uses them in a profane manner has transgressed, and even if it were unintentional he requires forgiveness, how much more so when dealing with a commandment enshrined in law for us by God, one may not trample on them simply because we do not understand their reason. (*Hilchot Me'ilah* 8:8)

Chapter 4

Laws Created by Rabbinic Legislation

INTRODUCTION

By definition, the origin of Sinaitic Law is certain; on the other hand it is not always certain what purpose the laws were intended to serve, because God's reason for mitzvot is not normally revealed. However, they have to be obeyed, because they are God's command.

Takkanot and *Gezerot* – the two types of Rabbinic legislation – are different in this respect. Their date of origin is not always certain, and the source of our obligation to observe them is not quite clear. On the other hand, it is generally possible to establish the purpose which they were intended to serve. The main issues to be considered in this chapter are when and why the major *Takkanot* and *Gezerot* were enacted, and the nature of the obligation to observe these enactments.

SECTION I: THE AGE OF THE MAJOR RABBINIC ENACTMENTS

Enactments of the Pre-Mishnaic Era

The Talmud reports the authorship of some isolated *Gezerot* and *Takkanot* and goes back as far as Moshe Rabbenu to whom it attributes "many *Gezerot* and *Takkanot*."[1] Important decrees are attributed to, among others: Yehoshua;[2] King David;[3] King Shlomo;[4] Ezra;[5] the *Anshei Knesset haGedolah* (the Men of the Great Assembly), to whom we are indebted for the Purim festivities;[6] Yochanan, the High Priest;[7] Yose ben Yoezer[8] and his colleague Yose ben Yochanan; and, the *Bet Din* of the *Chashmonaim*, to whom we owe the Festival of Lights, Chanukah.[9] It will be noted that all these *Gezerot* and *Takkanot* preceded the Mishnaic era, which began with Hillel and Shammai.

1. *Shabbat* 30a. For example, the seven days of marriage festivities and the seven days of mourning for the dead (*Talmud Yerushalmi, Ketubot* 1:1), the first blessing of Grace after Meals (*Berachot* 48b), and the obligation to preach and study the laws of a festival during the festival (*Megillah* 32a) are all attributed to Moshe Rabbenu.
2. There are ten *Takkanot* ascribed to Yehoshua in connection with the Land of Israel, for example: it is permissible for small cattle to pasture in large private woods; springs emerging for the first time on private land may be used by all the townspeople; anyone may fish in Lake Tiberias; and, paths that cross through private land may be used by the public until the second rain (*Eruvin* 17a). Yehoshua also instituted the second blessing of the Grace after Meals (*Berachot* 48b) and confirmed a *Gezerah* against intermarriage with *Netinim* (*Yevamot* 79a).
3. King David promulgated a *Gezerah* against *yichud* with an unmarried woman (*Avodah Zarah* 36b), and the third blessing in Grace after Meals is attributed to him (*Berachot* 48b).
4. Of King Shlomo it is said that he instituted the *eruv,* which permits carrying from a private domain into a courtyard after he himself had made the *Gezerah* prohibiting this. He also made a *Gezerah* declaring person's hands unclean for touching holy things (*Shabbat* 14b).
5. Among the *Gezerot* of Ezra was one penalizing the Levites by depriving them of their right to the tithes, because they did not return to Eretz Yisrael from the exile (*Yevamot* 86b). Among his *Takkanot* was one that required courts of law to sit on Mondays and Thursdays (*Bava Kama* 82a), and another *Takkanah* required that the Torah be read in public on Sabbath afternoon.
6. The *Anshei Knesset haGedolah* were also responsible for the *Amidah* prayer.
7. Yochanan, the High Priest, decreed that produce purchased from an *am ha'aretz* (unlearned person) must be assumed not to have been tithed. Also, that no hammer should strike in Jerusalem on *Chol haMoed* (*Sotah* 48a).
8. Yose ben Yoezer of Zereda and Yose ben Yochanan of Jerusalem declared impure all heathen countries, and also declared *tumah* (ritual impurity) on all glass utensils that are capable of becoming unclean (*Shabbat* 14b).
9. They also made a *Gezerah* against the teaching of Greek wisdom and the rearing of pigs (*Sotah* 49b).

In fact, it is claimed by R' Halevy[10] that all major *Takkanot* and *Gezerot* had been decreed prior to the era of Hillel and Shammai. R' Halevy, in developing the argument, relies mainly on the fact that the major Rabbinic decrees are not reported as having been instituted by any one particular person, but are reported anonymously and without dispute.

Anonymous Enactments of the Era of the Sanhedrin

As we have already explained,[11] when non-Sinaitic laws are reported anonymously, usually this indicates that they date back to the time when the Sanhedrin was in existence. Only when the Sanhedrin had ceased, and there was no forum where disputes could be settled, did the Halachah become subject to controversies, with the consequence that statements of *halachah* had to be attributed to individual sages or schools. According to R' Halevy,[12] the many *Takkanot* and *Gezerot* that appear anonymously and undisputed, are therefore likely to date back to the time of the Sanhedrin. Since, in fact, with very few exceptions, most major Rabbinic decrees are expressed anonymously and without controversy, it is reasonable to assume that by the time the Sanhedrin ceased to function – that is, by the beginning of the Mishnaic era – most major *Gezerot* and *Takkanot* were firmly established.

If, in order to take one set of Rabbinic laws as an example, we turn to the Sabbath laws, it will be found that "all the *Gezerot* which the Sages issued in connection with the restriction of work on the Sabbath are anonymous."[13] A very impressive list of such *Gezerot* can be produced. They include: the prohibition against setting food on a stove, because one might be tempted to stoke the fire;[14] a similar prohibition against covering up food with material that generates heat;[15] the prohibition

---

10. **Dorot HaRishonim* 1:3, p. 223, and see also p. 311 et seq.
11. See ante p. 12, footnote 38.
12. A similar view is expressed by *Maharatz Chajes, *Mavo HaTalmud*, p. 58. (See English edition, J. Schachter, tr. [New York, 1960].)
13. Maharatz Chajes, op. cit.
14. Mishnah *Shabbat* 3:1.
15. Ibid. 4:1.

against a woman going into the street wearing specified ornaments, because she might take them off and carry them, in order to show them to a friend;[16] the prohibition against a non-Jew doing work for a Jew;[17] the prohibition against the administration of justice, the conclusion of a betrothal or the transaction of a loan, because one might come to write;[18] the prohibition against swimming, because one might come to repair a swimming-vessel; the prohibition against examining accounts, for one might come to make notes;[19] and so on.

Enactments Disputed by the Early Tanna'im

Apart from the fact that they are stated anonymously there is another factor which indicates that many *Gezerot* pertaining to the Sabbath are of pre-Talmudic origin.[20] This is the fact that many *mishnayot* report disputes by the earliest *Tanna'im* concerning *details* in the application of such *Gezerot*. These early *Tanna'im* argue about the extent of these *Gezerot*, in which type of case they apply and under which circumstances they can be considered inapplicable – but even these first *Tanna'im* never call into question the existence of the *Gezerot*. It can therefore be safely assumed that the *Gezerot* themselves were of long standing by the beginning of the Mishnaic era, otherwise it would have been impossible for the earliest *Tanna'im* to have disputes about their details.

The oldest dispute recorded in the Mishnah, to which previous reference has been made,[21] may serve as an illustration of what has been stated. This dispute concerned the *Gezerah* of *Muktzeh*,[22] a prohibition which was directed against the handling of animals and other things not suitable for use on the Sabbath and *Yom Tov*. Here the Mishnah reports how the Sages, generations before the Talmudic era, argued whether this prohibition extended even to a case where the handling of animals was

16. Ibid. 6:1 and *Shabbat* 59b.
17. *Shabbat* 110a.
18. Mishnah *Beitzah* 5:2.
19. *Shabbat* 150a.
20. See **Dorot HaRishonim*, R' Halevy, op. cit. 1:3, p. 220 et seq., and p. 311 et seq.
21. See p. 12, footnote 38.
22. See p. 38, footnote 54.

required in order to comply with the ritual prescribed by the Torah for Temple offerings. The Sages, therefore, generations before the *Tanna'im,* already knew of the principle of *Muktzeh* and their controversy concerned only a detail in its application.

Similarly, early in the Mishnaic era there is a dispute recorded in the Mishnah[23] between Bet Hillel and Bet Shammai regarding the type of food which could be set on a stove on the Sabbath. In this Mishnah, as well, it is clear that both Bet Hillel and Bet Shammai knew the *Gezerah* against setting food on the stove on the Sabbath, and their dispute concerned only the question of how far this *Gezerah* extended.

As one final example, reference may be made to *Bameh Madlikin,*[24] the chapter of the Mishnah which, in some communities, forms part of the regular Friday night service. In that chapter, the Sages discuss which oils are permitted to be used for Sabbath lights and which are not permitted. This again shows that the principle of the *Takkanah* – that Sabbath lights have to be kindled – was well established beyond all disputes by the time of these *Tanna'im* and that only the *detail* as to which oils were to be used was open to question and doubt.

Rabbinic Enactments in the Mishnaic Era

What has been said of *Gezerot* and *Takkanot* concerning Sabbath laws is typical of Rabbinic laws. They usually appear anonymously and it must be assumed that they had, for the most part, been concluded by the beginning of the Talmudic era. Nevertheless, mention is made in the Talmud of *Gezerot* and *Takkanot* that were decreed by individual *Tanna'im* or their schools. For example, the Talmud reports *Gezerot* in the name of Hillel and Shammai and their schools after them. Bet Hillel and Bet Shammai[25] were said to have introduced thirty-six *Gezerot,* on eighteen of which their two schools were agreed, while

23. Mishnah *Shabbat* 3:1.
24. Mishnah *Shabbat* 2:1. See Ra'avad, *Sefer HaKabbalah.* It may be useful to add here that even when a certain *Takkanah* is attributed to one of the Sages, it may date back to a much older established custom which the Sage in question merely re-affirmed. See A. Korman, *Mavo l'Torah sheBichtav v'sheBe'al Peh* (Tel Aviv, 1966), p. 47 et seq.
25. See *Shabbat* 15a.

the remainder followed the view of Bet Shammai only. Yehoshua ben Gamla "is remembered for good," because he introduced the *Takkanah* of elementary education in all cities,[26] and R. Yochanan ben Zakkai, who after the Destruction of the Temple had to guide the people in their tragic circumstances, has to be mentioned for his *Takkanot* and *Gezerot* mainly "as a remembrance of the *Bet haMikdash*."[27] The record of Rabbinic decrees continues with those of R. Eliezer ben Azariah,[28] R. Gamliel of Yavneh,[29] the Sages at Usha[30] and others too numerous to specify. The fact, however, remains that all those *Takkanot* were on matters of detail; the broad basis of Rabbinic legislation had been laid many centuries earlier, long before the time of the Mishnah or the Talmud.

26. *Bava Batra* 21a.
27. R. Yochanan ben Zakkai decreed that buildings should not be built and painted like royal palaces, and that one should leave a square *amah* undecorated over (or opposite) the inside of the entrance of any building. He prescribed signs of mourning in connection with a woman's jewelry, the bridegroom's appearance, and the setting of places at meals (*Bava Batra* 60b). Also among the *Takkanot* of R. Yochanan was one that permitted the blowing of the *shofar* on Rosh Hashanah when it coincided with the Sabbath provided that there was a *Bet Din* in that locale, as well as one that the *lulav* should be used for seven days during the festival of Sukkot (*Rosh Hashanah* 31b).
28. On the day that R. Eliezer ben Azariah was appointed *Nasi,* it was decreed that the scrolls of *Kohelet* and *Shir HaShirim* should render hands unclean – thus putting those scrolls on an equal footing with the remainder of the Holy Writ.
29. R. Gamliel of Yavneh invalidated the *shechitah* of a Samaritan (*Chullin* 5b) and introduced an additional blessing in the *Amidah* (*Nedarim* 28b).
30. Named after one of the meeting places of the Sages in the middle of the second century (see *Ketubot* 49b). Their enactments include a decree that not more than a fifth of one's income may be given to charity. They also include a number of decrees concerning family law, such as a provision that parents must support their small children and that a son must support his father in a case where the latter has transferred all his property to him.

SECTION II: THE PURPOSE OF RABBINIC LEGISLATION

Enactments Which Experience Had Shown Necessary

The reasons for some *Takkanot* and *Gezerot* are quite apparent, because they were enacted to cure a specific mischief – frequently not hypothetical, but one that had occurred in practice. For example, the Sages required the dating of a *get* (bill of divorce) as a result of a case in which a husband, in order to save his adulterous wife, took advantage of an undated *get*. He gave her an undated *get* after her act of adultery and dated it prior to the act, so that to the *Bet Din* she appeared to be an unmarried woman at the relevant time.[31]

The Rabbinic prohibition against taking a hot bath on the Sabbath is another example. At one time, this was permissible, provided, of course, that the bath water had been heated before the Sabbath. The Rabbis found, however, that the bath attendants were heating water on the Sabbath and, when challenged, would claim that they had done it on the previous day. The Sages, accordingly, prohibited the taking of hot baths on the Sabbath.[32]

The Sages also found that people in certain occupations were particularly exposed to temptation, and they therefore stepped in to provide preventive legislation. They prohibited the purchase of wool, milk or kids from herdsmen, and the purchase of wood or fruit from those whose job was to watch over fruit trees.[33]

Although we have no definite evidence for this, it is probable that most *Gezerot* and *Takkanot* followed as the result of actual events which proved the need for special legislation. For example, it is probable that the thirty-nine types of work, which are prohibited by Sinaitic Law, proved, in the course of time, insufficient to achieve the ideal of a holy Sabbath day. Therefore, Rabbinic prohibitions like those directed against conducting business and the handling of *Muktzeh* objects had to be enacted in order to ensure that the Sabbath day was restored to

31. *Gittin* 17a and *Talmud Yerushalmi, Gittin* 4:3.
32. *Shabbat* 40a.
33. Mishnah *Bava Kama* 10:9.

its position as a holy day, set aside for study and prayer and for family and friends. It is likely that later generations did not have the same self-discipline as their ancestors had at the time of Sinai and, consequently, men who were engaged in business – which was permitted by Sinaitic Law – came to write and carry and do many other things which Sinaitic Law prohibited. Hence the Sages stepped in with preventive legislation creating a fence around the Torah – a fence which, in order to protect the Torah, had to become more extensive as the people became more lax in their observance.

The Four Objects of Rabbinic Enactments

While it is difficult to establish historically what motivated the Sages to enact any given decree at any particular time, the underlying purpose of *Gezerot* and *Takkanot* in general is not hard to discover. Their purpose is perhaps best summed up by Rabbi N.S. Greenspan, the late Principal of the London Yeshivah Etz Chaim, who said[34] that *Gezerot* were intended to guard against the transgression of a mitzvah, and *Takkanot* were intended to improve and advance one of the following:

1. Religion
2. Family
3. National consciousness
4. Society

Here it should be noted that just as the Torah never restricted its teachings and laws to matters of "religion" in the narrow sense, but was concerned with every aspect of life, so, too, the Rabbis were concerned in the course of their legislation with every aspect of Jewish life – whether secular or religious. They legislated against dealing in weapons or animals which were unsafe,[35] just as they legislated against dealing in food which was not kosher.[36] They prohibited the consumption of food which

34. **Melechet Machshevet* (London, 1955), p. 134 et seq.
35. Mishnah *Avodah Zarah* 1:7.
36. Mishnah *Shevi'it* 7:3.

had been exposed to serpents and snakes,[37] just as they prohibited food which had been cooked on the Sabbath.[38] Hence, while the Sages made provisions for the advancement of religious life by instituting the reading of the Torah in public, blessings and prayers, and so on, they were equally concerned with the advancement of the family, of the nation and of society. Some examples of Rabbinic decrees intended to serve those purposes will be mentioned by way of illustration.

The *Takkanot* in the sphere of family law laid particular emphasis on the welfare of the woman. *Takkanot* were enacted to protect the interests of young girls, who were to take precedence over their brothers in matters of inheritance and who could never be altogether disinherited.[39] The position of the married woman was also secured by many *Takkanot*,[40] and the general rabbinic principle was that "a man is to love his wife like himself and to honor her even more."[41] Even minor details did not escape attention; for example, Ezra instituted "that peddlers of cosmetics should call in all towns, so that cosmetics should be readily available and a wife should not be unattractive for her husband."[42] Further *Takkanot* protected the divorced woman and the widow.[43] On the other hand, there were *Takkanot* that regulated the duty of a woman towards her husband,[44] and finally, *Takkanot* that regulated the duty of parents to their children and vice versa.[45]

Of the enactments intended to promote national consciousness, Chanukah and Purim are the best known, but there were many other special days which had been set aside to commemorate God's deliverance of His people out of the enemy's hands. On the other hand, there were days of remembrance for national catastrophes, and above all there

---

37. Mishnah *Chullin* 2:5 and Mishnah *Terumot* 8:4, 5.
38. *Shabbat* 15a.
39. In other words, unmarried daughters were entitled to maintenance out of the inheritance (*Shulchan Aruch, Even HaEzer* 112).
40. A husband is obliged to pay for his wife to be healed from sickness or redeemed from captivity (*Ketubot* 51a), and to arrange for her funeral (ibid. 46b).
41. *Yevamot* 62a.
42. *Bava Kama* 82a.
43. *Talmud Yerushalmi, Ketubot* 11:3; *Ketubot* 95b.
44. *Ketubot* 46b.
45. *Kiddushin* 29a; *Ketubot* 65b; see also p. 64, footnote 30 ante.

were *Takkanot* like those of R. Yochanan to commemorate the Destruction of the Temple.

Enactments for the welfare of society included the various *Takkanot* instituted to regulate claims in civil law and the collection of debts, and the many *Takkanot* instituted for the sake of peace and equity.[46] The Sages were particularly concerned to establish proper standards of honesty. They extended the definition of "theft" to include gambling with dice and pigeon-racing;[47] taking an animal caught in a trap that had been set by another person;[48] attracting a swarm of bees away from its owner;[49] the gathering by one poor man of the olives which had been shaken from a tree by another.[50]

Takkanot and Gezerot Distinguished

In conclusion, it must be stated that while there is no cause to quarrel with R' Greenspan's definition of the aims of Rabbinic legislation, not all are agreed to the distinction he draws between *Takkanot* and *Gezerot*. As stated earlier, according to R' Greenspan, the former were enacted in order to further one of the four causes which have been mentioned, whereas the latter were enacted solely to guard against the transgression of a mitzvah.

Maharatz Chajes[51] is among those who take a different view. He claims that *Gezerot* are enactments that are negative in the sense that they prohibit certain actions, whereas *Takkanot* are positive in the sense that they require actions to be taken.

Although the view of Maharatz Chajes is generally followed, it does create difficulties. There are, in fact, a number of instances in the Talmud in which a negative prohibition is described as a *Takkanah*. For instance, the prohibition against re-marrying one's wife after hav-

46. *Gittin* 59a–b.
47. *Sanhedrin* 25b.
48. Mishnah *Gittin* 5:8.
49. Mishnah *Bava Kama* 10:2.
50. Mishnah *Gittin* 5:8.
51. Op. cit.

ing divorced her on account of her bad repute,[52] and against purchasing Jewish ritual articles from Gentiles, where the price charged is excessive,[53] are described as *Takkanot,* whereas according to the definition of Maharatz Chajes, they should have been described as *Gezerot,* because they are negative in nature. If, on the other hand, R' Greenspan's definition is followed, these cases present no difficulty. The prohibition against remarrying a woman divorced on account of her bad repute is properly described as a *Takkanah,* because it tends to promote family welfare. Similarly, the prohibition against purchasing ritual articles from Gentiles at excessive prices is properly described as a *Takkanah,* because it tends to promote national consciousness by preventing foreign exploitation.

SECTION III: THE OBLIGATION TO OBSERVE LAWS CREATED BY RABBINIC LEGISLATION

As mentioned earlier,[54] the obligation to observe the laws produced by the Sages in *interpreting* the Torah is based upon the verse: "If there be any matter too hard for you in judgment.... You shall come to the Priest, the Levite, and to the judge that shall be in those days, and inquire...you shall observe to do according to all that they inform you."[55]

Scriptural Authority for Rabbinic Legislation

It is generally accepted that *Takkanot* and *Gezerot,* too, have the force of law and the question will be asked, "From what source do these decrees of the Sages derive their force and validity?"

52. *Gittin* 45b.
53. Ibid.
54. See p. 34.
55. *Devarim* 17:8–10.

The View of Rambam

In his *Sefer HaMitzvot*,[56] Rambam states that Rabbinic decrees have the sanction of law, because the Torah declares them to be binding. The quotation from *Devarim* cited above concludes with the words "you shall observe to do according to all that they inform you," and Rambam states that this imposes a binding duty to observe all Rabbinic legislation.[57]

This view causes some difficulty. Previously, we explained[58] that there are a number of differences between (*d'Oraita*) Torah legislation and (*d'Rabanan*) Rabbinic legislation. It has been said that a person who is in doubt whether he has already fulfilled a certain legal duty, for example whether he has already listened to the shofar, will be obliged to listen to the shofar for what may be a second time, because this is a duty imposed by the Torah. If the duty concerned is one imposed by Rabbinic legislation, as for instance the obligation to wash ones hands before eating bread, he is not obligated in similar circumstances to wash his hands for what may be a second time.

The Objection of Ramban

It will be objected that if the obligation to observe Torah law and also the obligation to observe Rabbinic Law both flow from the Torah, there should be no distinction between the two types of law. Consequently, there would be no justification for the rule that laws which have the status of *d'Oraita* have to be treated more strictly and laws which have the status of *d'Rabanan* have to be treated with greater leniency. This criticism is made by Ramban in his commentary on *Sefer HaMitzvot*.[59]

In fact, however, as Ramban himself remarks, this objection may be overcome. The objection rests on the assumption that because the

56. **Shoresh* 1. See also *Hilchot Mamrim* 1:2.
57. In this, Rambam follows a view expressed in the Talmud, **Shabbat* 23a.
58. See p. 35, and footnote 40.
59. **Shoresh* 1.

Jewish People entered into a covenant at Sinai to observe all the mitzvot of the Torah, all mitzvot of the Torah comprised in that covenant must have equal status. By way of explanation, the duty to observe the Sabbath, the duty to observe the dietary laws, and the duty to listen to the Sages are of equal binding force. Either every mitzvah must be observed even by a person who is in doubt whether he has complied with it, or no mitzvah need be observed by a person in that position. This assumption, however, is not necessarily so. The duty to listen to the Sages depends upon *what* the Sages have decreed. If, therefore, the Sages themselves decreed that a person who is in doubt whether a Rabbinic obligation applies to him (like the person who is not sure if he properly washed his hands for bread) is freed from any obligation, then surely the duty to listen to the Sages is limited by what the Sages have themselves decreed.

Accordingly, a person who is in doubt whether he has properly performed the mitzvah of *netilat yadayim* for bread is freed from the obligation to wash again, not because the duty to listen to the Sages is of a lower status than the duty to observe the Sabbath, but because the duty to listen to the Sages must be taken to its logical conclusion. If one is obliged to listen to the Sages, one is obliged – or entitled – to listen to the Sages even when they say that a person who is in doubt whether he has properly performed *netilat yadayim* need not wash again.

A View That Rabbinic Enactments May Not Express the Will of God

The author of *Meshech Chochmah*[60] has a completely different approach. He questions the assumption that laws with the same source of obligation must have the same degree of obligation.

He claims that there is a different degree of obligation for laws specifically given at Sinai and for laws which were authorized at that time but were not then specified. This is so because the former laws express the Will of God, Whose will it is that the Sages are to be obeyed, as

60. *Commenting on *Devarim* 17:11.

much as that the Sabbath and the dietary laws are to be observed. His Will, however, is not specifically concerned that one's hands should be washed before eating bread. By way of analogy, he argues that whereas God made it a mitzvah to obey the king and it is His Will that the king be obeyed, it cannot be said that every command of the king expresses the Will of God.

This view, that only the general mitzvah of listening to the Sages coincides with the Will of God, but that the individual mitzvah ordained by the Sages – for example washing one's hands for bread – does not necessarily coincide with the Will of God, is not shared by R' Elchanan Wasserman.

A View That Rabbinic Enactments Always Express the Will of God

In *Kuntres Divrei Sofrim,*[61] R' Elchanan Wasserman, one of Lithuania's great Talmudists of the inter-war period, considers the view of Ramban that the obligation to observe Rabbinic decrees is not imposed by the Torah, and asks why, according to this view, Rabbinic laws are binding.[62] He suggests that Rabbinic laws have to be observed because they express the Will of God.[63] In this view, the Will of God is not concerned merely that the Sages shall be obeyed in a general sense, but it is the Will of God that *netilat yadayim* be performed before eating bread because when the Sages decreed any specific act, they revealed that it is God's Will that this act shall be done.

In conclusion, R' Wasserman proposes that the Will of God as expressed by Rabbinic legislation is of a lesser status than the Will of God which is expressed in the Scripture or in Sinaitic laws, and that it

61. *Baranowitz, 1924, p. 6.
62. The obligation cannot rest on any Sinaitic commandment or on "logic," otherwise it will be open to the very objection Ramban had raised against Rambam – namely, that Rabbinic laws should be of equal status with Torah laws.
63. Great men can anticipate and reveal the Will of God. See *Shabbat* 88b.

is this lower status of the mitzvah which accounts for the fact that when in doubt a person need not observe Rabbinic legislation.

This view that Rabbinic legislation expresses the Will of God puts *mitzvot d'Rabanan* in a new light.

Rabbinic Legislation Seen in a New Light

Rabbinic legislation gives rise to a conundrum which may be put as two questions:

1. If God did not consider the legislation necessary and did not make it part of the Torah given at Sinai, why did the Sages think it so? (This question can be asked for example about *Muktzeh* – Rabbinic law prohibiting handling certain objects on the Sabbath, e.g. tools normally used for work that is not allowed on the Sabbath.)
2. If certain pieces of Rabbinic legislation are clearly so appropriate, why in fact was it not part of Torah legislation at the time of *Matan Torah*? (This second question can be asked, for example, about *chinuch*.[64] The mitzvah of *chinuch* is a Rabbinic law requiring a father to educate his child in religious practice. So it may be asked: Why was it in order according to Sinaitic Law to leave a child without Jewish education of any sort? And how was the child suddenly at the age of thirteen to become an observant Jew?[65])

The answer to both questions may well be found in the words of Rabbi

---

64. The duty of *chinuch* is generally regarded as *d'Rabanan*. See *Sukkah* 2b, *Yoma* 82a. Some authorities consider *chinuch* to be *divrei Kabbalah* – see *Turei Even*; *Chagigah* 6a; *Chayei Adam, klal* 10:1. Others say there is a general duty *d'Oraita* to bring up a child *"b'darkei yashar"* ("in the correct manner"), but that teaching the details of mitzvot is *d'Rabanan* – see Rabbenu Mano'ach, *Shvitat Asur* 2:10.

65. A similar question may be asked regarding a blind man whose duty to observe mitzvot is only *d'Rabanan*. Before the Sages imposed this obligation, how was he to feel part of the Jewish People? See *Kiddushin* 31a and *Bava Kama* 87a.

Yeshayahu haLevi Horowitz (known as the Shlah haKadosh), who writes:[66]

> The Sages produced new things (laws) or through *pilpul*, but all that was in the potential of the voice [from Sinai] and the time had come to bring this from the potential to the actual... God commanded 365 prohibitions to fight the poison of the *Nachash* (a symbol of the *yetzer ha-ra).* As the poison increases, the generations require further prohibitions...had the situation been so at the time the Torah was given, these prohibitions would have been in the Torah...but they are really included in the prohibitions of the Torah because they are all of the same nature. That is why God commanded: *Asu mishmeret l'mishmarti*...so that any stringencies added in later generations are all of *d'Oraita* status.

If we now consider the problem of *Muktzeh* legislation in the light of the Shlah's remarks, it would appear that in earlier times the people were on a higher spiritual level and would not be at risk of transgressing Sabbath prohibitions, even without the preventive legislation of *Muktzeh.* While later generations required legislation – and it would be the Will of God to provide such legislation – in order to assure the correct conduct. This would answer the first question.

With regard to the example we used in the second question, we can say that the Torah never tolerated that a child should go without *chinuch.* It was the Will of God that there should be *chinuch.* However, *chinuch* legislation was not necessary in earlier times, because a father would educate his child under the age of thirteen as a matter of course. A Divine command was unnecessary. It was only later that the "poison of the *Nachash*" increased and the Will of God had to be specified in concrete legislation.

Both Torah and Rabbinic legislation can now be seen in a new light. The duty of *chinuch* and the laws of *Muktzeh* and all Rabbinic laws

66. *Shnei Luchot HaBrit* (Amsterdam, 1698), *Bet Chochmah* 28:2.

have the same source as all mitzvot – namely the Will of God. In fact, the Will of God can find expression in four different forms:

1. The *Taryag* (613) mitzvot[67]
2. The text of the Torah and its interpretation through the Sages[68]
3. *Halachah l'Moshe miSinai*
4. Rabbinic legislation

67. There are halachic consequences of a *d'Oraita* law being included in *Taryag* rather than being a law derived by interpretation. Specifically, (i) the latter do not result in *malkut* punishment (see *Pri Chadash, Petichah Kolelet, Orach Chayim* 1:2; also *Mitzvot Hashem* [Frankfurt, 1857], p. 108, *klal* 17); and (ii) hermeneutic rules may not be used to interpret them (see *Shabbat* 132a; Rashi, ad loc. s.v. "*uAkiva*"). For general discussion see A.H. Rabinowitz, *Taryag* (Jerusalem, 1978), p. 28 et seq.
68. There need not be an express command in the Torah in order to create a Torah obligation – e.g. the obligation to show gratitude; see *Igrot Moshe, Yoreh De'ah* 2:128.

Hebrew Sources

SECTION I

All Major Takkanot and Gezerot Pre-Date Hillel and Shammai

10. R' I.I. Halevy, Dorot HaRishonim 1:3, p. 223

כי אם שגם בנוגע לכל יסודי דרבנן לכל התקנות והכוללות, הנה לא לבד שכולם כבר זמנם האחרון הוא זמן אנשי כנסת הגדולה לפני ימי שמעון הצדיק כי אם שכבר אז גם נקבעו בכל יסודותיהם.

12. Maharatz Chajes, Mavo HaTalmud, p. 298

הרבה גזירות נמצא אצלנו במשנה סתם, ולא נחלק בהם אדם מעולם, ולא נוכל לברר מאיזה זמן בוא אלינו, ומתי עמדו חכמי הדור למנין על גזירות אלו, ובלי ספק כולם באין אלינו מן ב"ד הגדול, אשר נגזרו מהם במעמד שלם, אחר שעמדו עליהם למנין.

20. R' I.I. Halevy, Dorot HaRishonim 1:3, p. 220

כירה שהסיקוה בקש ובגבבא נותנין עליה תבשיל. בגפת ובעצים לא יתן עד שיגרוף או עד שיתן את האפר.

בית שמאי אומרים חמין אבל לא תבשיל ובית הלל אומרים חמין ותבשיל.

בית שמאי אומרים נוטלין אבל לא מחזירין ובית הלל אומרים אף מחזירין. (שבת ג א).

והדבר ידוע שכל איסור הטמנה אינו אלא מדרבנן ודברי בית שמאי ובית הלל אינם הולכים בנוגע להאיסור, כי אם בנוגע לההיתר, היינו בנוגע לפרטי דברי ההיתר האמורים במשנה. שעל זה שנאמר במשנה בהיתר התקנה כשהתנור גרוף וקטום, על זה יאמרו ב"ה שהכונה שאז כבר מותר לגמרי בכל האופנים. וב"ש סוברים שאז הותר בדין המשנה רק חמין אבל לא תבשיל. וגם זה רק ליטול אבל לא להחזיר.

SECTION II

The Purpose of Rabbinic Legislation

34. Rabbi N.S. Greenspan, Melechet Machshevet (London, 1955), p. 135

אם המטרה היא שלילית הרחקה מן העברה, תקון זה הוא "גזירה" ואם המטרה היא חיובית, בין שצורת התיקון היא אזהרה, בין שהיא צווי חיובי, קום ועשה, תקון זה נכנס אל סוג "התקנות". ועצם ההבחנה בין גזירה לתקנה חשוב מאד לדינא כאשר יתבאר בס"ד. התקונים החיוביים ביחס להמטרה החיובית שאליה שאפו המתקנים, שונים הם ובכללם אתה מוצא ארבעה: תקונים בחיים הדתיים, בחיים הלאומיים, בחיי המשפחה ובחיי החברה.

SECTION III

The Obligation to Observe Laws Created by Rabbinic Legislation

56. Rambam, Sefer HaMitzvot, Shoresh 1

השרש הראשון שאין ראוי למנות בכלל הזה המצות שהן מדרבנן:

דע כי זה הענין לא היה ראוי לעורר עליו לבארו, כי אחר שהיה לשון התלמוד (מכות כ"ג) תרי"ג מצות נאמרו למשה בסיני איך נאמר בדבר ההוא שהוא מדרבנן שהוא מכלל המנין, אבל העירונו עליו מפני שטעו בו רבים ומנו נר חנוכה ומקרא מגילה מכלל מצות עשה...

ומה שיראה לי שהביאם אל זה היותנו מברכין אשר קדשנו במצותיו וצונו ושאלת התלמוד (שבת כ"ג) היכן צונו ואמרו מלא תסור. ואם מטעם זה מנו אותם הנה ראוי שימנו כל דבר שהוא מדרבנן כי כל מה שצוונו חכמים לעשותו וכל מה שהזהירונו ממנו כבר צוה משה רבינו ע"ה בסיני שהוא צונו לעשותו והוא אמרו "על פי התורה אשר יורוך וגו'". והזהירנו יתברך מעבור דבר מכל מה שתקנו אותו או גזרו ואמר לא תסור. וגו'.

57. Shabbat 23a

אמר רב המדליק נר של חנוכה צריך לברך... מאי מברך? מברך אשר קדשנו במצוותיו וצונו להדליק נר של חנוכה. והיכן צונו? רב אויא אמר "מלא תסור" (דברים י"ז). רב נחמיה אמר "שאל אביך ויגדך זקניך ויאמרו לך" (דברים ל"ב).

59. Ramban, Shoresh 1

וכללו של דבר שדברי סופרים חלוקים הם בכל דיניהם מדברי תורה להקל באלו ולהחמיר באלו. ואם היה העובר על דבריהם או שאינו מקיים מצות שלהם עובר על עשה ועל לא תעשה היה חומר גודל בהם ולא היה ראויין לקולות הללו, ...ואולי תתעקש לדעת הרב כי מה שאמרו בכל מקום להקל בדברי סופרים הוא במחילה ובתנאי מאתם שהם התנו בגזירות ובסייגים שעשו לתורה וכן המצות שלהם שנלך בהם לקולא כדי לחלק ולהפריש בין מה שהוא דבר תורה ובין מה שהוא מדבריהם אע"פ שבכל אנו מצווין מן התורה. ולא היו ספיקות שבדבריהם ראויות להתיר אותן אלא מפני התנאי הזה שעשו בהן בתחלתן. ואין אלו דברים הגונים ולא של עיקר...

ומ"מ כללי הרב משתבשין אבל הדבר האמיתי המנוקה מכל שבוש הוא שנודיע שאין הלאו הזה לא תסור אלא במה שאמרו בפירוש התורה כגון הדברים הנדרשים בגזירה שוה או בבנין אב ושאר שלש עשרה מדות שהתורה נדרשת בהן או במשמעות לשון הכתוב עצמו וכן במה שקבלו הלכה למשה מסיני תורה שבעל פה... אבל הגזירות והתקנות שעשו חכמים למשמרת התורה ולגדר שלה אין להם בלאו הזה אלא סמך בעלמא.

60. Meshech Chochmah on Devarim 17:11

האמת כדברי רמב"ם, והעיקר הוא זה, כי התורה רצתה אשר מלבד ענינים הנצחים והקיימים לעד, יתחדש ענינים, סייגים, ואזהרות, וחומרות אשר יהיו זמניים, היינו שיהיה ביד החכמים להוסיף עפ"י גדרים הנמסר להם, ואם יעמוד ב"ד אחר גדול בחכמה ובמנין ובהסכם כלל ישראל, כפי הגדרים שיש בזה, הרשות בידם לבטל, ולמען שלא ימצא איש אחד לאמר אני הרואה ואינני כפוף לחכמי ישראל, נתנה התורה גדר לא תסור כו' שאל"כ יהיה תורה מסורה ביד כ"א, ויעשו אגודות... ואם כן המצוה דוקא לשמוע מה שיאמרו, אבל הענין בעצמו מה שאמרו וחדשו, אפשר דאינו מתקבל אל רצון הבורא... ורצה דוקא שמשמע בקולם אבל לא בפרטי הדברים. ומצאנו דוגמתו בתורה ענין דומה לזה, מה שהחמירה תורה לשמוע בקול מלך... ובכל זה לדוגמא שמעי בן גרא היה מצוה מן השם לשמוע בקול שלמה, לבלי לצאת מקיר העיר וחוצה וחייב מיתה ע"ז, אבל האם רצה השם שיאמר זה שלמה?...

ככה שמה התורה לחוק לבנ"י לשמוע בקול חז"ל כקול מלך, מאן מלכי רבנן. אבל בפרטי הענין אין רצונו בצווי פרטי.

ומעתה נבאר כל השגותיו, כי מספקא לן בדברי תורה, שמא הוא חזיר... א"כ אכלנו חזיר דבר המתועב באמת, אבל בספר עירוב, א"כ כיון שענין הזה אינו בפרט רצון הבורא, רק שצוה לשמוע אליהם, וכיון שע"ז לא דברו, א"כ לא נקרא מי שאינו עושה כן, שאינו שומע בקולם.

61. Kuntres Divrei Sofrim (Baranowitz, 1924), p. 6

נראה מדברי הרמב"ן, ממה שהוכיח מדמצינו שדבריהם קלין יותר מדאורייתא שלדבריו אין בדבריהם שום דאורייתא כלל. דאם נאמר שהרמב"ן לא חלק על הרמב"ם רק לענין קרא דלא תסור, אבל גם הוא מודה שנצטוינו מן התורה לשמוע לדברי חכמים מקרא או מסברא או מהלכה למשה מסיני. אם כן הקושיות שהקשה על הרמב"ם מפני מה דבריהם קלין משל תורה, נאמר לו ולטעמיה גם כן יקשה זאת הקושיא בעצמה. ומה נפקא מיניה, בזה אם נצטוינו לשמוע לדברי חכמים מקרא "דלא תסור" או מקרא אחרינא או מהלכה למשה מסיני ...אלא ע"כ צ"ל לכאורה לדעת הרמב"ן שלא נצטוינו כלל מן התורה לשמוע לדברי חכמים.

ותימה גדולה לומר כן, דאם כן מאיזה טעם אנו חייבין לשמוע להן?...

יש לומר בכל המצוות והאיסורין של דבריהן הסכימה דעתן לדעת המקום... ומהאי טעמא אנו חייבין לעשות כדבריהן, שהרי אנו מקיימין בזה רצון השי"ת שהסכימה דעתן לדעתו, ומכל מקום, כיון שלא בא עליהן ציווי מפורש בתורה הן קלין מדברי תורה המפורשין.

Chapter 5

Torah min haShamayim and Rabbinic Interpretation and Legislation

INTRODUCTION

The Written Law and the Oral Law are "one and the same Divine Law." This is what Rav David Zvi Hoffman writes in his famous essay on the Mishnah,[1] and then he goes on to say: "The Mishnah is for the greater part of Divine origin." So the Oral Law is all Divine Law, but it is only "for the greater part" of Divine origin – not in its entirety.

One is entitled to ask: Can a law be Divine when it is not of Divine origin? This cannot be dismissed as merely a matter of semantics – as we shall see, it touches on fundamental principles of faith. We shall proceed to investigate how Rambam defines *Torah min haShamayim*, the Talmudic term for laws of Divine origin – or Sinaitic Law, as we have termed it in this book.

1. *The First Mishna* (New York, 1977). (English translation of *Die Erste Mischna*.)

Rambam, in setting out his well-known Thirteen Principles of Faith, writes:[2]

> The eighth principal is *Torah min haShamayim:* That is, we believe that all the Torah that is in our possession today is the Torah which was given to Moshe from God...that he [Moshe] was like a writer who receives dictation.
>
> This statement relates to the Written Law.

Rambam then explains how the principal of *Torah min haShamayim* applies to the Oral Law. He writes:

> Also *Perush haMekubal* (the received commentary to the Written Torah) is from God. The fact that today we make a *sukkah, shofar, lulav, tzitzit, tefillin,* etc., in a certain form is because this is the form given by God to Moshe and he passed it on to us.

There is no claim here that the words of the Mishnah or Talmud are the words of God, given to Moshe, "like a writer who receives dictation"; it is rather the ideas and the content that is of Sinaitic origin.[3]

Rambam speaks only of *Perush haMekubal* (the received commentary to the Written Torah) – and not of the entire Oral Law – as being of Divine origin. It is important, therefore, to establish what comes under the category of *"Perush haMekubal"*?

---

2. **Sanhedrin, Perek Chelek* (Introduction).
3. We would suggest that this distinction has an effect in practical Halachah. In *Shulchan Aruch haRav* (*Hilchot Talmud Torah* 2:12–13) it states: "If one says the words (in learning Torah) although one does not understand their meaning, because one is an *am ha'aretz* (ignoramus), even so he has fulfilled the mitzvah of *talmud Torah.* However, this applies only to *Torah sheBichtav*; in the case of *Torah sheBe'al Peh,* if he does not understand the meaning of the words, he has not done any *limud* whatsoever." Surely, this is because in the case of *Torah sheBichtav* the words are God's words, hence they are *limud*; whereas in the case of *Torah sheBe'al Peh,* the ideas, but not the words, are from God. Hence, to say the words without understanding them is without value.

We have seen[4] how, according to Rambam, the Sages made their contributions to the Oral Law in three distinct and disparate ways:

1. By passing on the tradition from Sinai which had come down to them
2. By interpreting the law by means of *drash* and *svara* (logic) where there was no Sinaitic interpretation available
3. By legislating, by means of *Takkanot, Gezerot,* and Rabbinic mitzvot.

Traditions from Sinai were clearly *Perush haMekubal.* Rabbinic legislation was clearly not so. Interpretations by means of *drash* and *svara* are not so readily classifiable.

SECTION I: INTERPRETATIONS BY THE SAGES AS DIVINE LAW

Drash and Svara

On the one hand, Rabbinic interpretations had the status of *d'Oraita* Law;[5] yet on the other, by definition, they originated with the Sages, rather than at Sinai. Could they be part of *Perush haMekubal,* and if not, are they considered to be Divine Law?

As has been seen, the main vehicles for interpretation were *drash* and *svara. Drash* normally followed rules (*Middot*) which were of Sinaitic origin. It could be argued that laws produced by *drash* are therefore *Perush haMekubal.* Even if one argues that *drash* is not *Perush haMekubal,* it is certainly Divine Law. A similar argument can be advanced for laws based on logic, particularly where these follow as a logical necessity[6] from other laws which are of Sinaitic origin.

---

4. See ante p. 13.
5. See ante p. 35–36.
6. An example of "logical necessity" is: "If A is bigger than B and B is bigger than C, then A is bigger than C."

   Sometimes *svara* is good and sound sense, rather than logical necessity – e.g. *hapeh she'asar hu hapeh shehitir* (credibility to prohibit is credibility to permit), see **Ketubot*

It appears from the following passage that the Talmud[7] accepts *svara* and *drash* as Divine Law:

> One who maintains that the entire Torah is from Heaven with the exception of a particular vocalized spelling (*dikduk*) or a particular argument from major to minor (*Kal vaChomer*) or a particular textual analogy (*Gezerah Shavah*) – he is included among those who have "despised the word of God" (*Devarim* 15:31).[8]

Similarly, Rambam writes:[9]

> There are three types of *"kofrim b'Torah"* (deniers of Torah).... And also whoever does not accept the interpretation of the Scriptures, that is to say *Torah sheBe'al Peh* and whoever disputes the reliability of the bearers of tradition.

Rambam appears to be equating the Sages in their function as bearers of tradition with their function as interpreters, i.e. where the Sages produced laws by means of *drash* and *svara*.

22a: If a person is the only witness to create an *issur* (prohibition), he must also be believed if he creates a *heter* (permission) in the same matter. For example, if a man is the sole source of evidence that his daughter is married, he must also be believed if he identifies his daughter's husband, with whom she is accordingly permitted to live.

7. *Sanhedrin 99a.
8. It could be argued that this Talmudic statement is limited to *Gezerah Shavah* and *Kal vaChomer* as far as *drash* and *svara*, respectively, are concerned. Whether it applies similarly to all *drash* and *svara* is not clear. It may be argued that *Gezerah Shavah* is different, being one of the 13 *Middot* of *drash*, which particularly requires a tradition (*kabbalah*) – *Ein Adam dan Gezerah Shavah me'azmo* (*Pesachim* 66a). *Kal vaChomer*, however, is different; there is a principle: *Adam dan Kal vaChomer me'azmo* (*Niddah* 19b). This, therefore, presents a problem.

   See *Dikdukei Sofrim* who has different reading in this text. According to this it is a person who denies the authenticity of the 13 *Middot* – rather than a particular *drash* – who is condemned. See also *Margoliot HaYam*, ad loc.
9. **Hilchot Teshuvah* 3:8.

The Moral Svara

There is good authority for saying that the moral reasoning of the Sages was based on a moral sensitivity gained from the Written Torah – the Bible and the teachings of the prophets – and the ethical teachings[10] comprised in the Talmud, particularly in *Masechet Avot.* Indeed, Reb Ovadia MiBartenura says[11] that *Avot* starts with the statement "Moshe received the Torah at Sinai" in order to emphasis that the moral teachings of *Avot,* like other *halachot* in the Talmud, are of Sinaitic origin. So, there are good grounds for saying that laws based on interpretations by the Sages by means of *drash* and *svara* are Divine Law, in the sense that they express the Will of God.[12]

SECTION II: RABBINIC LEGISLATION AS DIVINE LAW

Takkanot and Gezerot

We turn next to *Takkanot* and *Gezerot.* There can be no doubt that for Rambam *Takkanot* and *Gezerot* are not *Perush haMekubal.* He writes:[13]

> There are not to be counted [among the 613 mitzvot] those which are of Rabbinic origin. You should know that it should not be necessary to point this out, because it is obvious. The Talmud says expressly that 613 mitzvot were related to Moshe at Sinai; how then can we say that a law of Rabbinic origin is part of this

10. *Imitatio Dei* is also a source of morality. See *Sotah 14a: "What is the meaning of 'You shall walk after the Lord your God'? Is it possible for a man to walk after the *Shechinah*...? But the meaning is: Follow the attributes of God. As He clothes the naked, so should you clothe the naked; as He visits the sick, so should you visit the sick; as He comforts the mourners, so should you comfort those who mourn."

    See also *Meshech Chochmah* on *Devarim* 30:12. Moral values are implanted by God in the conscience of man.
11. *Commenting on Mishnah *Avot* 1:1.
12. By way of illustration, when Rava ruled that one cannot kill an innocent person even to save one's own life, he was, in fact, saying that this was so intended by God when He commanded: "You shall not kill" (*Shemot* 20:13).
13. **Sefer HaMitzvot, Shoresh* 1.

> number? The reason why we point this out is that many were mistaken about this and counted the lighting of Chanukah lights and the reading of the *Megillah* among the positive commandments.... How can you say they were said to Moshe at Sinai? ...the Chanukah lights were legislated by the Sages at the time of the Second Temple – and the same remarks apply to the reading of the *Megillah*. Now, to say that these were indeed said to Moshe at Sinai, that he should command us that if, at the end of the Jewish Commonwealth, the Greeks would come and the following would happen, we must then kindle lights on Chanukah – I think that this is something that no one would imagine...

How then can Rabbinic legislation – a substantial part of the Oral Law – be Divine Law? We have referred to the view that Rabbinic legislation expresses the Will of God; there are, however, a number of additional arguments which support the proposition that Rabbinic legislation is part of Divine Law.[14]

God Informed Moshe of All the Detailed Rabbinic Legislation

If we carefully study the words just quoted above from *Sefer HaMitzvot*, it will be noted that Rambam says merely that Moshe was not commanded to tell the Children of Israel regarding, for example, a future duty to kindle Chanukah lights.

Rambam does not say that Moshe *himself* was not told about the future mitzvah.[15] In fact, as we have seen, according to the Talmud, "Moshe knew all the laws that would develop throughout the generations."[16]

---

14. In this connection, it is relevant to recall that laws were made by men inspired by *ruach hakodesh*. See ante p. 2 and footnotes.
15. See p. 10 for the views that Moshe did not hand down all the Oral Law he had received or was, in fact, not permitted to do so.
16. See pp. 20–21 for references and other Talmudic statements supporting this proposition, particularly *Megillah* 19b which concludes "God showed Moshe... the mitzvah of reading the *Megillah*."

The Torah Obligates Us to Observe Rabbinic Legislation

We have discussed the view of Rambam that all *d'Rabanan* laws have the backing of Written Law.[17] According to Rambam, one who flouts a Rabbinic law transgresses God's command not to deviate from the words of the Rabbis.[18] This gives Divine backing to Rabbinic legislation.

Rabbinic Legislation Is the Result of Logic *(Svara)*

In the previous chapter, we have considered in detail the view of R' Elchanan Wasserman that Rabbinic legislation expresses the Will of God (*ratzon Hashem*).[19] Here we note the view of R' Shimon Shkop,[20] who argues that all *mitzvot d'Rabanan* "were introduced for a good reason." It is not arbitrary that the Rabbis told us, for example, to kindle Chanukah lights or to read the *Megillah*. The Sages must have considered it to be a *svara*[21] to perform these mitzvot.[22]

---

17. See ante p. 70 et seq. for a full discussion.
18. "You shall observe to do according to all that they inform you" (*Devarim* 17:10), and: "...you shall not depart from the words that they shall tell you" (ibid. 17:11).
19. See ante p. 72 et seq.
20. **Kovetz Biurim, Shev Shmatese* 9.
21. Although *svara* can impose a *d'Oraita* obligation. Rabbi Shimon Shkop considers that this type of *svara* was not strong enough to impose an obligation of a *d'Oraita* status. However, the Rabbis consider it a sufficiently strong *svara* to impose an obligation of *mitzvot d'Rabbanan*.
22. We would suggest that the *svara* proposes that Hashem requires the performance of this particular mitzvah. It is, for example, the Will of God that Chanukah lights be kindled or that the *Megillah* be read, to mark the respective events – in which case the view of R' Shimon Shkop is almost identical to that of R' Elchanan Wasserman.

    It must be pointed out, however, that not all authorities agree that *mitzvot d'Rabanan* are the Will of God. There are those who argue that God wants us to obey the Sages – but that does not mean that He wants the specific action that the Sages had decreed (see pp. 71–72). To keep to the example previously used, God does not necessarily want Chanukah lights to be kindled; rather, He wants us to obey the Sages' decree – whatever it may be – and it so happens that they have decreed the kindling of Chanukah lights. This may well make a valid halachic difference (see *Netivat HaMishpat* 234).

D'Oraita and d'Rabanan – a Difference of Degree

In summary, it may be said that the two types of Oral Law – that which is *d'Oraita* and that which is *d'Rabanan* – are different only in degree, but not different in kind, as both are expressions of God's Will. In the case of laws received through the chain of tradition from Sinai, it is God Who revealed His Will; in the case of laws resulting from interpretation – and also in the case of Rabbinic legislation – it was the Sages who revealed the Will of God. Therefore all, as Rav Hoffman rightly says, are Divine Law.

Hebrew Sources

SECTION I

Torah min haShamayim

2. Rambam, Sanhedrin, Perek Chelek

והיסוד השמיני היות התורה מן השמים, והוא: שנאמין כי כל התורה הזו המצויה בידינו עתה היא הנתונה על ידי משה רבנו עליו השלום שהיא כולה מפי הגבורה כלומר: שהגיעה אליו כולה מאת ה׳ יתברך בענין שנקרא על דרך השאלה: ״דבור״ ואין יודע היאך הגיעה אלא הוא משה, עליו השלום, שהגיע לו. וכי הוא היה כמו סופר שקוראין לו וכו׳

Torah as Good Sound Sense

6. Ketubot 22a

גמ׳ א״ר אסי מנין להפה שאסר הוא הפה שהתיר מן התורה שנאמר את בתי נתתי לאיש הזה לאשה לאיש אסרה הזה התירה ל״ל קרא סברא היא הוא אסרה והוא שרי לה אלא כי איצטריך קרא לכדרב הונא אמר רב דא״ר הונא אמר רב מנין לאב שנאמן לאסור את בתו מן התורה שנאמר את בתי נתתי לאיש הזה למה לי מיבעי ליה לכדתני ר׳ יונה דתני ר׳ יונה את בתי נתתי לאיש הזה הזה ולא ליבם ת״ר האשה שאמרה אשת איש אני וחזרה ואמרה פנויה.

Divine Law

7. Sanhedrin 99a

ואפילו אמר כל התורה כולה מן השמים חוץ מדקדוק זה מקל וחומר זה מגזרה שוה זו זה הוא כי דבר ה׳ בזה.

9. Rambam, Hilchot Teshuvah 3:8

שלשה הן הנקראים אפיקורסין. האומר שאין שם נבואה כלל ואין שם מדע שמגיע מהבורא ללב בני האדם והמכחיש נבואתו של משה רבינו והאומר שאין הבורא יודע מעשה בני האדם כל אחד משלשה אלו הן אפיקורוסים שלשה הן הכופרים בתורה. האומר שאין התורה מעם ה׳ אפילו פסוק אחד אפילו תיבה אחת אם אמר משה אמרו מפי עצמו הרי זה כופר בתורה וכן הכופר בפרושה והוא תורה שבעל פה והמכחיש מגידיה כגון צדוק ובייתוס והאומר שהבורא החליף מצוה זו במצוה אחרת וכבר בטלה תורה זו אע״פ שהיא היתה מעם ה׳ כגון ההגרים כל אחד משלשה אלו כופר בתורה.

Torah Morality

10. Sotah 14a

ואמר רבי חמא ברבי חנינא מאי דכתיב אחרי ה׳ אלהיכם תלכו וכי אפשר לו לאדם להלך אחר שכינה והלא כבר נאמר כי ה׳ אלהיך אש אוכלה הוא אלא להלך אחר מדותיו של הקב״ה מה הוא מלביש ערומים דכתיב ויעש ה׳ אלהים לאדם ולאשתו כתנות עור וילבישם אף אתה הלבש ערומים הקב״ה ביקר חולים דכתיב וירא אליו ה׳ באלוני ממרא אף אתה בקר חולים הקב״ה ניחם אבלים דכתיב ויהי אחרי מות אברהם ויברך אלהים את יצחק בנו אף אתה נחם אבלים הקב״ה קבר מתים דכתיב ויקבר אותו בגיא אף אתה קבור מתים.

11. Bartenura, Mishnah Avot 1:1

אומר אני לפי שמסכת זו אינה מיוסדת על פירוש מצוה ממצות התורה כשאר מסכתות שבמשנה אלא כולה מוסרים ומדות וחכמי אומות העולם ג״כ חברו ספרים כמו שבדו מלבם בדרכי המוסר כיצד יתנהג האדם עם חבירו לפיכך התחיל התנא במסכת זו משה קבל תורה מסיני לומר לך שהמדות והמוסרים שבזו המסכתא לא בדו אותם חכמי המשנה מלבם אלא אף אלו נאמרו מסיני.

SECTION II

Rabbinic Legislation

13. Rambam, Sefer HaMitzvot, Shoresh 1

השרש הראשון שאין ראוי למנות בכלל הזה המצות שהן מדרבנן. דע כי זה הענין לא היה ראוי לעורר עליו לבארו, כי אחר שהיה לשון התלמוד (מכות כג:): תרי״ג

מצות נאמרו למשה בסיני איך נאמר בדבר ההוא שהוא מדרבנן שהוא מכלל המנין, אבל העירונו עליו מפני שטעו בו רבים ומנו נר חנוכה ומקרא מגילה מכלל מצות עשה, וכן מאה ברכות בכל יום ונחום אבלים ובקור חולים וקבורת מתים והלבשת ערומים וחשוב תקופות ושמונה עשר ימים לגמור את ההלל. והשתכל ממי שישמע לשונם נאמרו לו למשה בסיני וימנה קריאת ההלל ששבח בו דוד עליו השלום את האל יתברך שצוה בה משה וכן נר חנוכה שקבעוה חכמים בבית שני וכן קריאת המגילה. אמנם היות נאמר למשה בסיני שיצונו כי כשיהיה באחרית ממלכתנו ויקרה לנו עם היונים כך וכך יתחייב לנו להדליק נר חנוכה, הנה איני רואה שאחד ידמה זה או יעלה במחשבתו.

20. R' Shimon Shkop, Kovetz Biurim, Shev Shmatese 9

והרמב״ן השיג, כיון דכל איסורין דרבנן בכלל ״לא תסור״ אם כן איך על מה קאי הציווי הזה. ויש לומר ד״לא תסור״ קאי על הדברים אשר אינן מפורשים בתורה וחז״ל אומרים שהוא דאורייתא, כגון דבר הנלמד בי״ג מדות והלכה למשה מסיני. אבל צריך עיון לדעת הרמב״ן, מאיזה טעם אנו מצווין לשמוע לדרכי חז״ל. ועוד קשיא לי טובא, הא סוף סוף גם הרמב״ן ז״ל מודה שמחוייבין אנו לקיים דברי חכמים ז״ל, ושהקב״ה ציוונו לשמוע בקולם, אם כן מה הרויח הרמב״ן אם איסורין דרבנן אינן בכלל ״לא תסור״, הא סוף סוף דאורייתא הוא, יהיה מאיזה טעם שיהיה, ואם כן האיך נקל בספיקותיהם. ודבר זה שאלתי מאת מורי הרה״ג ר׳ שמעון הכהן (שליט״א) [זצ״ל], והשיב לי, דלדעת הרמב״ן ז״ל מה שאנו צריכין לקיים דברי חז״ל הוא מן הסברא, דהא כל מה שאסרו חכמים הלא היה להם טעם מספיק על זה. ואם כן מן הטעם הזה בעצמו אנו מוזהרין שלא לעבור על איסורן, אלא שהטעם הזה אינו מספיק אלא לוודאן ולא לספקן. ולדוגמא, כשאסרו חז״ל שניות כדי להתרחק מן העריות, אם כן מן הטעם הזה אנו צריכים להתרחק מן משניות, אבל להתרחק בשביל זה מספק שניה, זה אין הסברא מחייבתנו ומשום הכי ספק שניה מותרת, עכ״ל. ודבריו ברורים למבין בכוונתה הרמב״ן.

Chapter 6

Restrictions on Rabbinic Legislation

INTRODUCTION

In the unequal partnership between Sinaitic and Rabbinic Law, the former played the dominant part and imposed limitations on the latter. Sinaitic Law restricted the manner in which the Sages were entitled to present their legislation and in general circumscribed the legislative powers of the Sages. These limitations are important in that they helped to preserve the Divine element in the Oral Law. They will be considered in three sections, which will show that:

1. Rabbinic legislation was not to be misrepresented as though it were inspired by prophecy;
2. It was not to be misrepresented as though it were Torah legislation;
3. Torah law and decisions of an earlier *Bet Din*, as well as the will of the people, imposed certain restrictions on the legislative powers of the Sages.

SECTION I: PROPHECY AND LEGISLATION

The Sages could not claim prophetic revelation as the source of their legislation, because once the Torah had been given at Sinai, prophetic revelation ceased to be relevant. The Torah had been given and it was unalterable. Even God Himself would not alter it.[1] What then could prophecy add to the Oral Law? Revelation was completed and now only interpretation could follow.

Rambam states the rule as follows: Because "the Torah is not in Heaven,"[2] a prophet cannot claim competence to produce new laws. Furthermore, even if the prophet states the law in accordance with Halachah, the fact that he claims prophetic inspiration as the source of his statement renders him a false prophet.[3]

Did the prophets, in fact, try to influence and change Halachah? To what extent do the early sources support the rules propounded by Rambam?

In the Talmud, there are conflicting authorities on the point. On the one hand the intervention in a matter of *halachah* by a heavenly voice – a *Bat Kol* – was completely rejected by R. Yehoshua.[4] It is also reported that both Yehoshua and later the prophet Shemuel refused to inquire in Heaven regarding forgotten *halachot,* because "no prophet may produce any new laws."[5] On the other hand, it is reported in *Masechet Megillah* that the prophets reestablished certain laws which had been forgotten."[6] However, the rule as propounded by Rambam is not, in fact, contradicted by the case in *Masechet Megillah.* A distinction must be drawn between the prophet acting in his capacity as a Sage and spiritual leader and the prophet acting as a man with a message from

1. *Rambam; the ninth of the Thirteen Principles of Faith as interpreted in the *Ani Maamin* Prayer.
2. *Bava Metzia* 59b.
3. Rambam, **Hilchot Yesodei HaTorah* 9:4; see *Kesef Mishneh,* ad loc.
4. **Bava Metzia* 59b, but see *Tosafot,* ad loc., that occasionally the decision of a *Bat Kol* is accepted, e.g. in the dispute between Bet Shammai and Bet Hillel. See p. 144. See also *Igrot Moshe* (by R. Moshe Feinstein) *Orach Chayim,* resp. #14.
5. **Temurah* 16a.
6. **Megillah* 2b and 3a.

God.[7] In the first capacity the prophet is under no disability; there is, accordingly, no objection to a prophet reestablishing forgotten laws, provided he does not act as a prophet, but relies on his wisdom and knowledge of the Torah.

Hora'at Sha'ah

Similarly, in his capacity as the spiritual leader of the people, the prophet was entitled to invoke the power of *Hora'at Sha'ah*. This power entitles the prophet or the *Bet Din haGadol* to suspend, in exceptional circumstances, the application of Torah law, provided:[8]

1. The suspension of the Torah law is not on a permanent basis.
2. The purpose of such suspension is to strengthen Torah law generally.[9]

The classical case of a prophet exercising the power of *Hora'at Sha'ah* is that of Eliyahu on Mount Carmel,[10] when, contrary to Torah law, he

7. This distinction is drawn by Maharatz Chajes in *Torat HaNevi'im, Eleh HaMitzvot*, Ch. 1.
8. Whether (1) and (2) are alternatives or cumulatives is not clear. Rambam stresses the temporary basis of *Hora'at Sha'ah* (see *Hilchot Yesodei HaTorah* 9:3). In **Yevamot* 90b, Rashi and Meiri stress only (2). The difference of opinion may hinge on the interpretation of the expression "*lefi sha'ah*" (*Yevamot*, loc. cit.). Does it mean temporary, or according to the requirement of the time, or both?
9. There is a further proviso that there is no authority to permit idol worship, even as *Hora'at Sha'ah* (Rambam, loc. cit.). According to the Talmud (*Yevamot*, loc. cit.) and *Sifrei* (*Devarim*, sec. 68), the doctrine of *Hora'at Sha'ah* is based on the words (*Devarim* 18:16): "You shall listen to him (i.e. the prophet)." Also *Tehillim* 119:126 is interpreted as giving authority to "destroy of His law because it is a time to act for God." See *Temurah* 14b; *Berachot* 54a and 63a; *Yoma* 69a and Rashi, ad loc.; and Kimchi commentary on *Tehillim*.
10. "Ahab sent among all the Children of Israel, and gathered the prophets together to Mount Carmel. And Eliyahu drew near to all the people, and said: 'How long will you go limping between two opinions? If the Lord is God, follow Him; but if Baal, then follow him.' And the people answered him not a word. Then Eliyahu said to the people: 'I, only, remain a prophet of the Lord; but Ba'al's prophets are four hundred and fifty men. Let them therefore give us two bullocks; and let them choose one

brought burnt-offerings outside the precincts of the Temple. But there were other such incidents,[11] like the offerings by Yehoshua at Mount Eval,[12] or by Gideon at the stronghold,[13] or by Manoach on the rock.[14] In all these cases, it appears that the Torah law which required sacrifices to be brought exclusively within the precincts of the Temple[15] was transgressed.

There are even instances recorded of the death sentence being executed contrary to established principles. For example the *Megadef*[16] was sentenced to death, although at the time of his offense the penalty had not been fixed. Achan[17] and the Amalekite[18] were both executed, although it was their own confession which convicted them. If the nor-

---

bullock for themselves, and cut it in pieces and lay it on the wood pile, and put no fire underneath. And I will prepare the other bullock, and lay it on the wood pile, and put no fire underneath. And call on the name of your gods, and I will call on the Name of the Lord. And whichever God answers by fire, He is the [true] God." (*Melachim* I 18:20-24).

11. See Maharatz Chajes, op. cit.
12. "Then Yehoshua built an altar to the Lord, the God of Israel, in Mount Eval...and they offered thereon burnt-offerings to the Lord, and sacrificed peace-offerings " (*Yehoshua* 8:30–31). See *Bemidbar Rabbah* 14:1.
13. "And it came to pass on the same night, that the Lord said to him: 'Take your father's bullock, and the second bullock of seven years old, and throw down the altar of Ba'al that your father has, and cut down the Asherah that is by it; and build an altar to the Lord your God upon the top of this stronghold, in the ordered place, and take the second bullock, and offer a burnt-offering with the wood of the Asherah which you shall cut down" (*Shoftim* 6:25–27). See *Temurah* 28b.
14. "So Manoach took the kids with the meal-offering, and offered it upon the rock to the Lord" (*Shoftim* 13:19). See *Zevachim* 119b.
15. *Devarim* 12:13.
16. "And the Israelite woman's son uttered blasphemously the name and execrated...And they placed him in ward, that the mind of the Eternal might be showed them. And the Eternal spoke to Moshe saying: 'Let all the congregation of Israel overwhelm him with stones'" (*Vayikra* 24:11–14). See Remah, *Sanhedrin* 78b; and *Divrei David* on *Vayikra* 24:12.
17. "And Yehoshua said to Achan: 'My son, give, I pray you, glory to the Lord, the God of Israel, and make confession to Him; and tell me now what you have done; hide nothing from me.' And Achan answered Yehoshua and said: 'Indeed I have sinned against the Lord, the God of Israel, and thus and thus have I done.'" (*Yehoshua* 7:19–20). See Abarbanel and Ralbag; and Rambam, *Hilchot Yesodei HaTorah* 9:3.
18. "And David said to the young man who told him, 'How do you know that Shaul and

mal Torah laws had been applied in any of these cases, the death penalty could never have been inflicted.

Although in some of these cases, there was an express command of God which required the prophet to act otherwise than in accordance with established law, the Tosafists[19] state[20] that such express authority from God is not essential for *Hora'at Sha'ah* to operate.

In these cases the prophet does not in fact act as a prophet, but rather with the same authority with which the *Bet Din haGadol*[21] was invested. The Talmud[22] reports a case in which the *Bet Din haGadol* invoked its power of *Hora'at Sha'ah.* This was during the Greek occupation of the Holy Land, when a man rode on a horse on the Sabbath. The *Bet Din* ordered him to be stoned. "This was done not because it was the proper punishment, but because the particular time required such action."

The Prophets and Temple Sacrifices

In dealing with prophecy and legislation, it is necessary to mention the often repeated allegation that the Prophets aspired to change the Biblical laws concerning Temple sacrifices.

The problem of the prophets and their attitude to Temple sacrifices, it has been pointed out, resolves itself upon a thorough examina-

---

Yonatan, his son, are dead?'... And he said to me: Stand, I pray you, beside me, and slay me, for the agony has seized me, and yet I still have life in me. So I stood beside him, and slew him..." (*Shemuel* II 1:5,9-10).

19. Tosafists were the authors of *Tosafot,* explanatory glosses on the Talmud. They were mostly of French and German origin and date from the twelfth and thirteenth centuries.
20. *Tosefot Yeshanim, Yevamot* 90b, s.v. "*Kemo*"; **Tosafot,* ad loc., s.v. "*V'ligmor*"; *Tosafot, Sanhedrin* 89b, s.v. "*Eliya*"; Meiri, ad loc.; *Minchat Chinuch,* Mitzvah 516; but according to *Minchat Chinuch,* Rambam does not share this view.
21. Rambam, Mishnah *Sanhedrin* 24:4 and *Hilchot Mamrim* 2:4. This power is limited to the *Bet Din haGadol* according to Ra'avad, *Hilchot Mamrim* 2:9; *Chiddushei haRan, Sanhedrin* 46a; *Nemukei Yosef, Sanhedrin* 52b; but it is not limited according to Meiri, *Sanhedrin* 52b; Rashba, *Responsa* 5:238 and *Tur Choshen Mishpat.*
22. **Yevamot* 90b.

tion of the relevant texts in the books of *Shemuel,*[23] *Yeshayahu,*[24] and the latter prophets.[25] It will become quite clear that these prophets did not object to the bringing of sacrifices, or to prayer, except by persons whose "hands are full of blood."[26] As Yirmeyahu said, "Will you still murder, commit adultery and offer unto Baal and walk after other gods whom you have not known and come and stand before Me in this house...?"[27] The prophets exclaim against persons who have sunk to the depths of moral wickedness and yet turn to God in prayer and Temple sacrifice.

In no case does a prophet protest against the observance of mitzvot by morally degraded people, other than prayer and sacrifice.[28] It has not been said by any of the prophets that God rejects the observance of mitzvot, such as the Sabbath or Pesach, by even the most wicked individuals.

A New Suggestion

We would suggest that the act of prayer and the bringing of sacrifices are different from any other mitzvot. They are intended to demonstrate something in relation to the person who observes these mitzvot – that he subjects himself to the rule of God.[29]

In the case of other mitzvot, this is not so. Mitzvot like the Sab-

---

23. "Has the Lord as great delight in burnt-offerings and sacrifices as in the obeying the voice of the Lord? Behold to obey is better than sacrifices and to hearken than the fat of rams" (*Shemuel* I 15:22).
24. "To what purpose is the multitude of your sacrifices to Me? says the Lord...I cannot endure iniquity along with the solemn assembly...even when you make many prayers I will not hear, your hands are full of blood" (*Yeshayahu* 1:11-15).
25. "For I desire mercy not sacrifices" (*Hoshea* 6:6). "Neither will I regard the peace-offerings of your fat beasts. Take away from Me the noise of your songs; for I will not hear the melody of your lutes. But let justice roll down like waters and righteousness like a mighty stream" (*Amos* 5:22-24). "Will the Lord be pleased with thousands of rams?" (*Michah* 6:7).
26. *Yeshayahu,* loc. cit.
27. *Yirmeyahu* 7:9.
28. The reference to the New Moon and the Sabbath (*Yeshayahu* 1:13) is to the sacrifices brought on those occasions (*Metzudat David,* ad loc.).
29. "What is the worship of the heart? – It is prayer" (*Ta'anit* 2a).

bath and Pesach demonstrate something about the creation of the world and about the Exodus from Egypt. They demonstrate facts which are true, quite independent of the character of the person who performs the mitzvah.

For a thief or a murderer to pray or to bring sacrifices, is therefore to demonstrate something which is a lie. A thief or murderer who observes the Sabbath or Pesach, on the other hand, still demonstrates something which is completely true.

The burden of the message of the prophets, accordingly, was not to change the mode of worship, but to change the mode of life of the worshipers.

SECTION II: THE PROHIBITION AGAINST ADDING[30] TO THE TORAH

Devarim 4:2 reads: "You shall not add to the word which I command you, neither shall you diminish from it."

This presents a problem. Does this not mean that all Rabbinic legislation is *ultra vires*? Yet the Talmud states that according to Biblical Law there is the positive obligation upon the Sages to protect God's commandments by means of legislation.[31]

However, a distinction must be drawn between adding to God's Laws and creating a new system of Rabbinic laws. By way of analogy it may be said that one does not add to the Empire State Building by erecting another building one hundred and two stories high, but by increasing the height of the existing building. Similarly, the Sages are not adding to God's laws by creating a body of Rabbinic legislation as they would be if they extended the laws of the Torah, for example, by adding an eighth day to Sukkot or by putting five fringes on the *tallit*.

30. The discussion which follows centers around the prohibition against adding to the commandments of the Torah *mutatis mutandis*; the same principles apply to the prohibition against detracting therefrom.

31. *Yevamot* 21a.

Two Ways of Adding to the Torah

Presenting *d'Rabbanan* Laws as *d'Oraita*

The prohibition against adding to the Torah would be relevant, however, had the Sages wanted to present their laws as if they were the laws of the Torah – to revert to our analogy, one may add to the number of Empire State Buildings if one erects another building of one hundred and two stories and calls the newly erected building by the same name. So, also, one may be adding to God's laws if one puts forward Rabbinic legislation as if it were God's command. Accordingly, Ramban[32] declares that the prohibition against adding to God's laws is not infringed, provided that "it is made clear that the particular laws have been made as a fence around the Torah and are not from the Torah." Likewise, Rambam[33] writes that the prohibition is not violated if the Rabbis declare unequivocally that what they ordain is of Rabbinic origin and do not treat their own laws as if they were Torah laws.

This then presents a restriction upon the manner in which the Sages could legislate; namely, that they could not claim the authority of the Torah laws for their own legislation.

Extending the *d'Oraita* Laws

The prohibition against adding to or detracting from Torah law would be relevant had the Sages wanted to extend the laws of the Torah by requiring the performance of a mitzvah at a time when, according to the Torah, it does not apply. For example, it prohibits the sitting in the *sukkah* for eight days when the Torah has prescribed that one should do so for only seven days.[34] It also prohibits the performance of a mitzvah with additional objects; for example, it prohibits the fixing of a fifth fringe to a *tallit* when the Torah has prescribed only four.[35]

---

32. Commenting on **Devarim* 4:2.
33. **Hilchot Mamrim* 2:9. Ra'avad, ad loc., disagrees. See also *Ohr Same'ach*, ad loc., and *Sefer HaChinuch*, Mitzvah 454.
34. *Rosh Hashanah* 28b.
35. *Sifrei, Devarim* 13:1, sec. 55; *Sanhedrin* 88b; Yosef Albo, *Sefer HaIkkarim* 3:14 states: "The Torah does not warn against adding to the number of mitzvot, but against

According to Rashba[36] these further restrictions did not apply to Rabbinic *Takkanot* and *Gezerot,* because they were enacted to protect Torah law;[37] so that, for example, the *Takkanah* of a second day of *Yom Tov*[38] was perfectly legitimate.

Other commentators[39] claim that in any event the second day *Yom Tov* does not constitute a contravention of the prohibition against adding to the laws of the Torah. They explain that the second day was not intended to add to the *Yom Tov* ordained by the Torah, but to make sure that the correct day was kept, and therefore both days were, in fact, observed with the intention of keeping the proper first day.

SECTION III: THE WILL OF GOD, THE WILL OF THE *BET DIN*, AND THE WILL OF THE PEOPLE

The Sages were further restricted in their legislative powers by:

- The will of God
- The will of the *Bet Din*
- The will of the people

---

adding something to the method of performing the mitzvot."

36. R' Shlomo ben Avraham Aderet, thirteenth-century Spanish Talmudist
37. *Rosh Hashanah* 16b.
38. It should be explained that a new month would be declared either after 29 days or after 30 days, in either case counting from the 1st day of the previous month. If the Sanhedrin in Jerusalem had received evidence on the 30th day that the New Moon had been seen, that day would be declared as the 1st of the next month, otherwise the following day would be so declared. Until they had received news from Jerusalem, a distant settlement did not know which of two days was the first of the month. Accordingly, in order to make sure of observing the correct day of *Yom Tov,* they had to keep *Yom Tov* on two days. This applied even to a *Yom Tov* that came only on the 15th of the month, because the news frequently took longer than 15 days to reach outlying areas.
39. See Rashi, *Eruvin* 96a and *Shiltei HaGiborim,* Mishnah *Rosh Hashanah* 4.

The Will of God

The will of God as expressed by Sinaitic laws was absolutely binding on the Sages. "Have then the Sages power to uproot this law of the Torah?" the Sages asked rhetorically.[40]

Yet, in exceptional circumstances, the Torah empowered the Sages to legislate contrary to Sinaitic Law. Exactly what these circumstances were is a matter of dispute between the great early scholars.[41] One rule, however, is clearly stated in the Talmud,[42] namely, that the Sages were entitled to decree that an action which the Torah required to be done, should *not* be done. They could prevent a person from carrying out an act required by the Torah, as distinct from requiring him to carry out an act prohibited by the Torah. The distinction which is made is one between an act of commission and an act of omission.

The Rabbinic prohibition against blowing the shofar when Rosh Hashanah coincides with the Sabbath is a case in point. The Torah had ordained that the shofar must be blown on Rosh Hashanah, and the Torah had made no distinction between Rosh Hashanah when it falls on a weekday and Rosh Hashanah when it coincides with the Sabbath. The Sages, however, were afraid that the shofar might come to be carried through the streets on the Sabbath, so they decreed that the law requiring the shofar to be blown on Rosh Hashanah shall not apply when Rosh Hashanah coincides with the Sabbath.[43]

As in the case of shofar, so also in all other cases[44] where the Sages decided to legislate against Torah law in the manner described, they did so in order to protect some other law against transgression. They thought it better that a law of the Torah should be allowed to go by default than that another law should be actively transgressed.

---

40. See **Gittin* 36a.
41. *Yevamot* 88a, *Tosafot*, s.v. *"Mitoch"* and *Nemukei Yosef* ad loc.
42. **Gittin* 36b.
43. **Rosh Hashanah* 29b.
44. See *Yevamot* 90b for six classical cases. See also Mishnah *Pesachim* 6:1, 8:8; *Shabbat* 130b; and Maharatz Chajes's *Darkei HaHora'ah*, II.

The Will of the Bet Din

A decision by the judges of an earlier *Bet Din* created a precedent that a later *Bet Din* was bound to follow. When a *Bet Din* had decided a question of *halachah* this decision became part of the body of the Oral Law, and no later *Bet Din* could reverse this decision "unless it was greater in wisdom and numbers."[45]

Even a change of circumstances would not automatically annul the decision of an earlier *Bet Din.*[46] For example, the Mishnah reports a Rabbinic decree prohibiting the redemption of the fruit of any four-year-old vineyard (*neta revai'i*) near Jerusalem. It had to be taken to Jerusalem and eaten there "so that the streets of Jerusalem should be decked with fruit"; this decree continued in force even after the Destruction of the Temple and even though there was no purpose in having the streets of conquered Jerusalem decked with fruit. Only when R. Yochanan and his *Bet Din* eventually abolished this decree was it again possible to redeem the fruit and take the money to Jerusalem instead.[47]

Where the Sages, in making a decree, had intended that it should cease to apply in changed circumstances, new circumstances render the decree obsolete, without any further action on the part of a *Bet Din.*[48] The Tosafists[49] claim that Rabbinic decrees like that against drinking uncovered water or that against trading with non-Jews on their holy days automatically ceased to apply when circumstances changed. This is so because the law against drinking uncovered water had been enacted in a time and in countries where snakes were prevalent, and the law against

45. *Mishnah *Eduyot* 1:5; Rambam, *Hilchot Mamrim* 2:2. Because the *Bet Din haGadol* never varied from the prescribed number of seventy-one members, "greater in numbers" cannot have its natural meaning and has been variously interpreted to mean that it has more sages following its decisions (Rambam, loc. cit.) or more pupils at its yeshivah (*Bartenura* on *Eduyot,* ad loc.) or even that it is presided over by an older *Av Bet Din* (*Tiferet Yisrael* and *Tosefot Yom-Tov,* ad loc.).

46. See *Beitzah* 5a, and Ra'avad's and Radbaz's comments on Rambam, loc. cit.; *Avodah Zarah* 36a; Rosh, *Responsa* 2:8; *Chiddushei haRan* on *Sanhedrin* 59b.

47. *Beitzah* 5b.

48. *Chiddushei Meiri, Avodah Zarah* 36a; *Pri Chadash* on *Yoreh De'ah* 116.

49. **Tosafot, Avodah Zarah* 35a, s.v. *"Chodo"*; *Ibid. 57b, s.v. *"Afukei"* but see **Pesachim* 50a, s.v. *"Makom"*

trading with non-Jews on their holy days had been enacted in times of idol worship, when non-Jews were wont to bless their idols for their good fortune. The Tosafists assume that when these laws were enacted they were never intended for different circumstances in other countries. These decrees, therefore, became obsolete, and the authority of a *Bet Din* was not required to abolish them.

The Will of the People

Finally, the will of the people restricted the legislative power of the Sages. Rambam expresses the rule thus: "Before instituting a decree or enacting an ordinance or introducing a custom which is deemed necessary, *Bet Din* must calmly deliberate and make sure that the majority of the community can live up to it. At no time is a decree to be imposed upon the public which the majority cannot endure."[50(א)] It is in this sense that the expression "will of the people" is used here. For example, the Sages were concerned that animals strayed into other people's fields and ate the crops. Accordingly, they decided to restrict the rearing of animals. However, out of consideration for the convenience of the people, they limited their restriction to sheep, which could be imported from other countries, and excluded cattle, which could not.[51] Again, in order to avoid hardship, the Sages refused to prohibit produce of a field which had been plowed during the Sabbatical year, because the majority of the people would be too severely affected by such a prohibition.[52] Similarly, they refused to decree excessive mourning for the Destruction of the Temple, because it was something which the majority of the people were unable to bear.[53]

In addition to the fact that the Sages could not enact laws which the people were unable to endure, if a law had not spread widely among

50. *Hilchot Mamrim* 2:5.
51. **Bava Kama* 79b.
52. *Talmud Yerushalmi, Shevi'it* 4:2; Tosefta, *Shevi'it* 3.
53. **Bava Batra* 60b.

the people,[54] it could be abolished by a subsequent *Bet Din*, even if that *Bet Din* was neither greater in numbers nor in wisdom.[55]

These three factors – the Will of God, the will of *Bet Din* and the will of the people – circumscribed the legislative powers of the Sages. However, before it can be said with finality that the Sages were strictly confined in their development of the Oral Law within this framework, one well-recognized legal device for affecting changes in the law other than by legislation has to be considered, and we shall turn our attention to this in the following chapter.

---

54. **Avodah Zarah* 36a. As to whether "a *Gezerah* that had not spread widely among the people" is a concept distinct from "a *Gezerah* that most people could not carry out" see Rambam, *Hilchot Mamrim* 2:3 and *Lechem Mishneh*, ad loc. Also Ran and Meiri, *Avodah Zarah* 36a.
55. There were in fact: (1) Decrees which only a greater *Bet Din* could abolish; (2) decrees which even a greater *Bet Din* could not abolish; and, (3) decrees which even a lesser *Bet Din* could abolish. According to some views the eighteen *Gezerot* of Bet Shammai and Bet Hillel belonged to the second group (*Talmud Yerushalmi, Shabbat* 1:4) – at least those of the eighteen *Gezerot* which had spread widely among the people. Those that had not so spread belonged to the last group. According to other views, all decrees which had spread widely among the people belonged to the middle group.

Notes of Rav Simcha Wasserman זצ״ל

א. זה משום שהוראה תלויה בבי״ד ומעשה תלוי בקהל.

Hebrew Sources

SECTION I

The Torah Is Not in Heaven

1. Rambam, Hilchot Yesodei HaTorah 9:4

וכן (נביא) אם עקר דבר מדברים שלמדנו מפי השמועה או שאמר בדין מדיני תורה שה׳ צוה לו שהדין כך הוא והלכה כדברי פלוני הרי זה נביא השקר ויחנק אע״פ שעשה אות שהרי בא להכחיש התורה שאמר לא בשמים היא. אבל לפי שעה שומעין לו בכל.

4. Bava Metzia 59b

מאי עכנאי אמר ר״י אמר שמואל שהקיפו דברים כעכנא זו וטמאוהו. תנא באותו היום השיב רבי אליעזר כל תשובות שבעולם ולא קבלו הימנו אמר להם אם הלכה כמותי חרוב זה יוכיח נעקר חרוב ממקומו מאה אמה ואמרי לה ארבע מאות אמה. אמרו לו אין מביאין ראיה מן החרוב. חזר ואמר להם אם הלכה כמותי אמת המים יוכיחו. חזרו אמת המים לאחוריהם. אמרו לו אין מביאין ראיה מאמת המים. חזר ואמר להם אם הלכה כמותי כותלי בית המדרש יוכיחו הטו כותלי בית המדרש ליפול, גער בהם ר׳ יהושע... יצאתה בת קול ואמרה מה לכם אצל ר״א שהלכה כמותו בכ״מ עמד ר״י על רגליו ואמר לא בשמים היא. מאי לא בשמים היא? אמר רבי ירמיה שכבר נתנה תורה מהר סיני. אין אנו משגיחין בבת קול שכבר כתבת בהר סיני בתורה ״אחרי רבים להטות״... אותו היום הביאו כל טהרות שטיהר ר״א ושרפום באש ונמנו עליו וברכוהו.

5. Temurah 16a

אף חטאת שמתו בעליה נשתכחה בימי אבלו של משה אמרו לפנחס שאל! אמר להם לא בשמים היא א״ל לאלעזר שאל! אמר להם אלה המצות שאין נביא רשאי לחדש דבר מעתה.

6. Megillah 2b

מנצפ"ך צופים (נביאי הדורות - רש"י) אמרום. ותסברא והכתיב "אלה המצוות" (ויקרא כ"ז) שאין נביא רשאי לחדש דבר מעתה? ... אלא שכחום וחזרו ויסדום.

Hora'at Sha'ah

8. Yevamot 90b

ת"ש "אליו תשמעון" (דברים י"ח) אפילו אומר לך עבור על אחת מכל מצוות שבתורה כגון אליהו בהר הכרמל הכל לפי שעה שמע לו? שאני התם דכתיב "אליו תשמעון". וליגמר מיניה? מיגדר מילתא שאני:

20. Tosafot ad loc., s.v. "V'ligmor"

וא"ת שאני התם דעל פי הדבור היה מתנבא לעבור והיכי נגמר מיניה לעבור משום תקנתא דרבנן שלא על פי הדיבור? ונראה דכיון דעל פי הדבור שרי משום צורך שעה, הוא הדין שלא על פי הדיבור, שהרי אין נביא רשאי לחדש דבר מעתה.

22. Yevamot 90b

א"ר אלעזר בן יעקב שמעתי שב"ד מכין ועונשין שלא מן התורה, ולא לעבור על דברי תורה אלא לעשות סייג לתורה. ומעשה באדם אחד שרכב על סוס בשבת בימי יונים, והביאוהו לב"ד וסקלוהו, לא מפני שראוי לכך אלא שהשעה צריכה לכך.

SECTION II

Rabbinic Laws Must Not Be Presented as Torah Laws

32. Ramban, Devarim 4:2

ומה שתקנו חכמים משום גדר כגון שניות לעריות וכיוצא בהן כי היא מצוה מן התורה ובלבד שידע שהם משום הגדר הזה ואינן מפי הקב"ה בתורה.

33. Rambam, Hilchot Mamrim 2:9

הואיל ויש לבית דין לגזור ולאסור דבר המותר ויעמוד איסורו לדורות וכן יש

להן להתיר איסורי תורה לפי שעה מהו זה שהזהירה תורה "לא תוסיף עליו ולא תגרע ממנו"? שאל להוסיף על דברי תורה ולא לגרוע מהן ולקבוע הדבר לעולם בדבר שהוא מן התורה בין בתורה שבכתב בין התורה שבע"פ כיצד הרי כתוב בתורה "לא תבשל גדי בחלב אמו". מפי השמועה למדו שזה הכתוב אסר לבשל ולאכול בשר בחלב בין בשר בהמה בין בשר חיה אבל בשר העוף מותר בחלב מן התורה, אם יבוא בית דין ויתיר בשר חיה בחלב הרי זה גורע. ואם יאסור בשר העוף ויאמר שהוא בכלל הגדי והוא אסור מן התורה הרי זה מוסיף. אבל אם אמר בשר העוף מותר מן התורה ואנו נאסור אותו ונודיע לעם שהוא גזרה... אין זה מוסיף.

The Prohibition against Adding to Torah Law Did Not Apply to Takkanot and Gezerot

37. Rashba, Rosh Hashanah 16b

הקשו בתוספות "והא קא עבר משום בל תוסיף?"

ומסתברא דלא קשי' כלל דלא אמרו התם דאיכא משום בל תוסיף אלא במה שהוא מוסיף מדעת עצמו כגון כהן שהוסיף ברכה משלו וא"נ ישן בשמיני בסוכה במתכוון למצוה וכיוצא באלו אבל במה שעמדו חכמים ותקנו לצורך אין כאן בל תוסיף דכבר נאמר על פי התורה אשר יורוך.

SECTION III

Rabbinical Law Must Not Contravene Torah Law

40. Gittin 36a

ומי איכא מידי דמדאורייתא משמטא שביעית והתקין הלל דלא משמטא?

The Sages Could Decree the Omission of an Act Required by Torah Law

42. Gittin 36b

ומי איכא מידי דמדאורייתא לא משמטא שביעית ותקינו רבנן דתשמט - אמר אביי שב ואל תעשה הוא.

43. Rosh Hashanah 29b

מתני׳: יום טוב של ר״ה שחל להיות בשבת, במקדש היו תוקעין אבל לא במדינה״...

גמ׳: מנה״מ... הכל חייבין בתקיעת שופר ואין הכל בקיאין בתקיעת שופר, גזירה שמא יטלנו בידו וילך אצל הבקי ללמוד, ויעבירנו ד׳ אמות ברשות הרבים והיינו טעמא דלולב והיינו טעמא דמגילה.

The Binding Force of a Bet Din Decision

45. Mishnah Eduyot 1:5

שאין בית דין יכול לבטל דברי ב״ד חבירו עד שיהיה גדול ממנו בחכמה ובמנין.

Decrees Which Were Not Intended to Apply in Changed Circumstances

49. Tosafot, Avodah Zarah 35a, s.v. "Chodo"

ואנו שאין נחשים מצוין בינינו אין לחוש משום גלוי. ואין לומר דדבר שבמנין הוא וצריך מנין אחר להתירו, כי ודאי הוא כשאסרו תחלה לא אסרו אלא במקום שהנחשים מצוין.

49. Tosafot, Avodah Zarah 57b, s.v. "Afukei"

ואע״ג דגם משא ומתן ביום אידם היה דבר שבמנין ולא הוצרך מנין אחר להתירו להנהו דלא אזלו ומודו כי ודאי מתחילה לא גזרו עליהם.

49. Tosafot, Pesachim 50a, s.v. "Makom"

מקום שנהגו לעשות מלאכה בערבי פסחים עד חצות עושין:... מאי שנא ערבי פסחים משאר י״ט? משום דזמן הפסח מחצות ואילך... ונראה דאף בזמן הזה דליכא הקרבה כיון שנאסר אז אסור לעולם.

The Will of the People

51. Bava Kama 79b

אף על פי שאמרו אין מגדלין בהמה דקה, אבל מגדלין בהמה גסה, לפי שאין גוזרין

גזרה על הצבור אלא אם רוב צבור יכולין לעמוד בה. בהמה דקה אפשר להביא מחוץ לארץ בהמה גסה אי אפשר וכו׳.

53. *Bava Batra 60b*
כשחרב הבית בשניה רבו פרושין בישראל שלא לאכול בשר ושלא לשתות יין. נטפל להן ר׳ יהושע אמר להן... בני בואו ואומר לכם, שלא להתאבל כל עיקר אי אפשר שכבר נגזרה גזרה. ולהתאבל יותר מדאי אי אפשר שאין גוזרין גזירה על הצבור אא״כ רוב הצבור יכולין לעמוד בה...

54. *Avodah Zarah 36a*
שמן, ר׳ יהודה ובית דינו נמנו עליו והתירוהו... ור׳ יהודה הנשיא היכי מצי למישרא תקנתא דתלמידי שמאי והלל, והתנן אין בית דין יכול לבטל דברי בית דין חבירו אלא אם כן גדול הימנו בחכמה ובמנין. ועוד הא אמר רבה בר בר חנה אמר ר׳ יוחנן בכל יכול לבטל בית דין דברי בית דין חברו חוץ משמונה עשר דבר... אמר רב משרשיא מה טעם? הואיל ופשט איסורו ברוב ישראל, שמן לא פשט איסורו ברוב ישראל... וסמכו רבותינו (רבי יהודה הנשיא - רש״י) על ... שהיו אומרים אין גוזרין גזרה על הצבור אא״כ רוב צבור יכולין לעמוד בה.

Chapter 7

Legal Fictions, the Spirit of the Law, and *Lifnim Mishurat haDin*

INTRODUCTION

It has been seen that there were severe restrictions on the legislative power of the Sages. In most legal systems comparable restrictions have produced the urge to find loopholes and to create devices which circumvent unwelcome limitations. When a change in the law was unattainable in the usual manner, resort was had to legal fictions, in order to produce by other means what could not be achieved by legislation. In this chapter, we shall investigate whether – in view of the limitations upon their power to legislate – the Sages in Jewish Law made use of similar devices.

First, what is a "legal fiction"? According to the *Concise Law Dictionary*[1] a legal fiction is "a statement *or* supposition which is known to be untrue, but which is not allowed to be denied in order that some difficultly may be overcome." Henry Sumner Maine, in his *Ancient*

1. Percy George Osborn (London, 1964), p. 6.

Law,[2] uses the term "legal fiction" in a wider sense to include "any assumption which conceals or affects to conceal that a rule of law has undergone alteration, its letter remaining unchanged and its operation being modified."

An example of a legal fiction in its more narrow sense from Roman Law is the *"manumission per vindictum"* which was a method whereby a slave could become free. It was "a fictitious suit, in which a person claimed that a slave was free-born. The master admitted the claim and the magistrate made a decree establishing the freedom of the slave."[3]

The imagination of the English jurists was equally fertile when, with the increase of international trade, the limits of territorial jurisdiction presented difficulties. "In order to meet the difficulty of contracts made beyond the seas, a fiction was adopted...the Writ alleged that the contract was a transaction made or entered into, according to the custom of merchants at the place where it was made, e.g. at Marseilles, and proceeded to add *'Apud Mary-le-Bow in Cheapside'* (a well-known location in London) or some other venue within the jurisdiction of the Common Law Courts."[4]

SECTION I: LEGAL FICTIONS AND *HA'ARAMOT* DISTINGUISHED

The *Ha'aramah* ("artifice") frequently met with in the Talmud closely resembles the legal fiction. It will be argued in this chapter, however, that often the *Ha'aramah* in Jewish Law was not used "in order that some difficulty may be overcome," or in order to conceal a change in the established law, but on the contrary, in circumstances where there was a danger of the established law being confused or forgotten, and the *Ha'aramah* was brought into play as a guard against that potential risk.

2. 1863, p. 25.
3. William Alexander Hunter, *Introduction to Roman Law* (London, 1908), p. 23.
4. Harold Potter, *Historical Introduction to English Law and Its Institutions* (London, 1958), p. 207.

Ha'aramot Which Do Not Circumvent the Law

The following examples of *Ha'aramah* illustrate this argument:

In *Masechet Shabbat,*[5] the Talmud considers what is to happen when an animal and its offspring have fallen down a well on *Yom Tov.* An animal cannot be moved on *Yom Tov,* because of the Rabbinic laws of *Muktzeh,*[6] unless it is required for its meat, in which case it may be handled for the purpose of slaughter. If this had been a case where only one animal had fallen down the well, the solution would have been a simple one. The animal could have been raised for the purpose of slaughter. In this case, however, there is a complication. The Torah prohibits the slaughter of an animal and its offspring on the same day,[7] and so it is not possible to raise both animals from the well for the purpose of slaughter. Consequently, R. Yehoshua suggests the following artifice, "Let him first raise one of the animals from the well in order to slaughter it and then not slaughter it.[8] He then raises the next animal, in order to slaughter that and he can, in fact, slaughter whichever one he likes.[9]

In this type of case, there is, in fact, an element of fiction. True, it is prescribed that the owner must, as he raises the animal, have the intention of slaughtering it. However, the "intention" is in conflict with his knowledge that he will change his mind.

In this case the *Ha'aramah* was not instrumental in effecting any change in the law or overcoming any difficulty in the law. Here, the position was that an animal was in distress, and the Torah expressly prohibits the causing of pain and distress to animals. Accordingly, the fundamental position in law is that the prohibition of *Muktzeh* does not apply to the case where an animal has to be handled in order to allevi-

5. **Shabbat* 117b.
6. See ante p. 38, footnote 54.
7. See *Vayikra* 22:28.
8. Rashi explains that he can make an excuse that he would rather see the other animal in case it is fatter.
9. There are a number of similar cases. See *Shabbat* 117b (saving property from fire); *Beitzah* 11b (salting meat on *Yom Tov*); and *Pesachim* 46b (taking *challah* when ritually unclean).

ate its distress.[10] However, R. Yehoshua requires the *Ha'aramah* as a reminder that in normal circumstances an animal must not be handled on *Yom Tov,* except for slaughter.

Our next example is from *Masechet Moed Katan*[11] where R. Yehudah rules that a scribe may write and sell *tefillin* and *mezuzot* during *Chol haMoed* provided he had originally intended them for his own use. He can, in fact, continually write *tefillin* and *mezuzot* for his own use and continually change his mind and sell them.

Here again, there is an element of fiction. As in the previous case, so here the "intention" of the scribe to use the *tefillin* for himself is in conflict with the "knowledge" that he will change his mind. And here again, the *Ha'aramah* plays no part in the legal process which in effect permits the scribe to write *tefillin* and *mezuzot* for sale. Fundamentally, the prohibition against writing for business purposes on *Chol haMoed* does not apply to the trade of a scribe who writes religious scrolls.[12] R. Yehudah requires the *Ha'aramah* however, as a reminder that under normal circumstances it is an infringement of the laws of *Chol haMo'ed* to write for business purposes.

It hardly requires to be pointed out that in any event the somewhat unreal "intention" in the two cases cited is a far cry from the complete fabrication involved in the legal fictions of Roman and English Law, like the affirmation that Marseilles is in Bow or that a slave is a free-man. "Intentions" in the sense of unspoken thoughts have no legal effect in Jewish Law[13] and in any event, the intention in the sense of "purpose" of an act is, of necessity, hard to nail down.

Former Israeli Supreme Court Judge Moshe Silberg, for example, describes[14] as a legal fiction the *Ha'aramah* of R. Tarfon,[15] a *Tanna* who was also a *kohen.* In time of famine, he married three hundred women so that they, as wives of a priest, would be able to eat *Terumah,* which was plentiful. We find it difficult to see why marrying a poor woman to

10. See Rambam, *Hilchot Yom Tov* 2:4.
11. **Moed Katan* 19a.
12. This is R. Yose's view, but he requires no *Ha'aramah.*
13. *Kiddushin* 49b: *"Devarim she'b'lev einam devarim."*
14. *Kach Darko shel Talmud* (Jerusalem, 1964), p. 26.
15. *Talmud Yerushalmi, Yevamot* 4:12.

save her from starving should be any more fictitious than marrying a rich woman to prevent oneself from starving. The "intention" or "purpose" is more noble in the one case than in the other, but does that render the marriage more fictitious?

The Pruzbal

Our final example is Hillel's famous *Pruzbal.* The Talmud[16] states that when Hillel found that people were not lending money to those in need for fear that the debts would be remitted in the Sabbatical year,[17] he ordained the *Pruzbal.* This was a document which the creditor made out and which stated that he handed over his debt to the *Bet Din* for collection. Once this document had been executed the debts were no longer remitted in the Sabbatical year.

This *Pruzbal* is considered a classical case of legal fiction, because there is a pretense that the debt has been assigned to *Bet Din*, when, in fact, nothing of the sort has taken place.

In fact, however, here again the *Ha'aramah* of *Pruzbal* plays no part in the process which permits the debt to be recovered after the Sabbatical year. This is made clear in the Talmud. The Talmud asks: "Has Hillel the power to abolish the laws applicable to the Sabbatical year?" and Rava replies that, in fact, the Sabbatical year continues to operate and so remit all debts. However, Hillel had made use of the power vested in the *Bet Din* to expropriate property when public policy required this. By virtue of this power, Hillel has expropriated the amount of the debt in the possession of the debtor and restored it to the lender.[18]

It will be noted that the *Pruzbal* played no part in this "expropriation." The power of expropriation had been enjoyed by every *Bet Din* since the days of Sinai[19] and required neither *Pruzbal* nor any document

16. **Gittin* 36a.
17. See *Devarim* 15:1-2: "At the end of every seven years you shall make a remission. And this is the manner of the remission: every creditor who lends anything to his neighbor shall remit it, he shall not exact it of his neighbor...."
18. This is the view of Rashi, ad loc., but see *Tosafot.*
19. Rabbi K. Kahana Kagan writes: "The right of expropriation by courts and communal leaders was incontestable. Rambam summarizes the general Rabbinic view by saying

or formality for its operation. The *Pruzbal* was instituted, however, so that it should not be forgotten, in those circumstances, that the Torah had provided for the remission of debts in the Sabbatical year.[20]

In fact, not all cases of *Ha'aramah* conform to this pattern. There are a number of cases where the *Ha'aramah* is not imposed in order to protect the normal law, but as a device which "enables some difficulty to be overcome or which allows the letter of the law to remain unchanged and its operation to be modified." Some of these cases will be discussed next. It will be noted that even in these cases there is no fictional pretense that something has taken place "which is not allowed to be denied." On the contrary, both law and fact are strictly observed in the cases which will be considered. Some say they are too strictly upheld, so much so that the spirit of the law is destroyed and the purpose of the law vitiated.

SECTION II: THE LAW AND THE REASONS FOR THE LAW

Do the many cases of *Ha'aramah* which are known to the Talmud destroy the spirit of the law? Why did the Sages not legislate to close loopholes in the law? Perhaps they did not originate the *Ha'aramot*, but why did they not put an end to them? These and similar questions have all been asked in connection with such *Ha'aramot* as conform strictly with the letter of the law, but which seem to vitiate the very result which the law was intended to produce.

---

that a judge may always expropriate money belonging to whom whatsoever, destroy it and give it away, if in his judgment this would serve to prevent the breaking down of defenses of the law or to strengthen its structure... This was one of the instruments for elasticity of the law. It was not the Rabbis themselves, however, who created this right of expropriation. They found source for it in the Bible" (*Three Great Systems of Jurisprudence* [London, 1955], p. 160).

20. In the previous two illustrations our interpretation of *Ha'aramah* is a tentative suggestion. In this case, however, this is how the *Ha'aramah* must be interpreted, if Rashi's view is followed.

Ha'aramot Which Circumvent the Law

Before attempting to answer these questions, let us consider some illustrations of this type of *Ha'aramah*. One such *Ha'aramah* is that which concerns tithe. In connection with tithe, the Talmud[21] suggests that since the obligation to give tithe arises only at the time when corn which has been winnowed is brought in by the front gate, it is possible to bring in the corn by the front gate *before* it has been winnowed, or not to bring it in through the front gate at all, and so escape the liability for tithe altogether.

In another case, the Mishnah[22] suggests a method of overcoming the task of carrying *ma'aser sheni* to Jerusalem without any additional expense. Normally, a person was entitled to redeem his own *ma'aser sheni* and take the money to Jerusalem instead. If he did this, he had to add one-fifth of its value.[23] One is also entitled to redeem another person's *ma'aser sheni*, and in that case there is no need to add a fifth. The Sages say: "A man may say to his son and daughter...'Here is money – you redeem the *maaser sheni*. By so doing, he can save himself the liability for the additional one-fifth.

If a poor man has made a vow not to derive any benefit from his benefactor and now finds that he has nothing to eat, the Sages say that the benefactor can give some food to a friend who may then pass it on to the poor man.[24]

The Mishnah[25] states that "one may not derive benefit from *chametz* which belongs to a Jew and which had been in his possession over Passover." *Chametz* belonging to a gentile is not prohibited for it is written: "Let it not be seen of *you*."[26] Now, states the Tosefta, if "a Jew and a gentile travel in a ship and the Jew has *chametz* in his possession, he can sell it to the gentile and buy it back after Passover."[27]

---

21. **Berachot* 31a.
22. *Mishnah *Ma'aser Sheni* 4:4.
23. See *Vayikra* 27:31.
24. *Mishnah *Nedarim* 5:6.
25. Mishnah *Pesachim* 2:2.
26. *Shemot* 13:17.
27. The sale must be an outright sale, *Tosefta, *Pesachim* 2:6. See also *Shulchan Aruch*,

Purpose in Law

These then are the types of *Ha'aramot* which rightly or wrongly have been described as "legal fictions" and which have given rise to the question why the Sages permitted these devices, which, while paying homage to the letter of the law, were designed to frustrate its purpose and spirit.

We would suggest that the answer is that Torah law is essentially different from other systems of law.

It is inappropriate to speak glibly of destroying the purpose and spirit of the Torah law, because, as will be shown, the reason or purpose of a law of the Torah is hardly ever certain and frequently entirely unknown. In such circumstances, it is not possible to speak of destroying the *spirit* – in the sense of the "purpose" – of a law.

The laws of the Torah are divided into two categories: one, *chukkim,* whose purpose cannot be understood, and the other, *mishpatim,* whose purpose appears self-evident. Yet even there, it must not be thought that one's own rationalization explains God's purpose. The Mishnah in *Masechet Megillah*[28] states that one must not refer in prayer to God's command to send away the mother bird before taking eggs from a nest, by saying "Your mercy extends to a bird's nest." The Talmud explains that it is wrong to say so, because God's commands are absolute decrees and not attributed to "mercy."[29]

Even where the reason for a law is clear, the Sages held that the law is not governed by its purpose.[30] For example, when the Torah speaks of the seven tribes which inhabited Canaan and states, "Neither shall you intermarry with them for they will turn away your sons...that they may

Orach Chayim 448:3 and *Mekor Chayim,* loc. cit. 11.

28. **Megillah* 25a; see also *Berachot* 33b.
29. See Asriel Rosenfeld, *Intercom,* Vol. III, no. 3.
30. In fact, the Sages stated (*Beitzah* 5a) that the Torah itself makes it clear that God's commands are not governed by their purpose. This is shown clearly by God's command at Sinai that all men must stay away from their wives for three days before the Torah was given (see *Shemot* 9:15). The purpose of this command was to make certain that the men would be ritually clean on that great day. After the Torah had been given, the purpose of the command had been spent and, therefore, if God's command were governed by its purpose, the men would have been entitled to return to their women without any further word from God. Here it is seen that the laws of

serve other gods."[31] R. Shimon argues[32] that this text must be construed as prohibiting all intermarriage – not only intermarriage with the seven tribes – because any marriage out of the faith presents the same danger. The Sages, however, did not heed this argument; they considered that the law cannot be governed by its purpose. These particular words of the Bible were directed against the seven tribes and must remain limited in that manner, although if one were to consider their purpose, all intermarriage should be brought within the ambit of the prohibition.[33]

Strict Interpretation

In view of what has been said, it is not possible to complain that *Ha'aramot* give rise to a too strict or too literal interpretation of the law and to claim that an interpretation in accordance with the so-called "spirit" of the law is called for. True, normally a law can be interpreted either strictly or in accordance with the purpose it was intended to serve. Where, however, as in most Torah laws, the latter possibility is ruled out, there is no alternative but to construe the law strictly.

Indeed there are endless examples of the law being construed in the strictest sense, even outside the realm of *Ha'aramah*. For example, the rule discussed in *Masechet Ketubot*[34] "A widow who has returned to her father's house after her husband's death must claim her *ketubah* entitlement within twenty-five years. Does it then depend on this? [asks the Talmud] – if she claims before sunset at the end of the twenty-five years, she gets her *ketubah* entitlement, and if after sunset, she forfeits it?" "Yes" is the answer given, and the Talmud goes on to explain that there are many cases in which the law is applied with equal stringency. In fact, examples can be supplied almost without limit.

---

the Torah are not governed by their purpose, because, in fact, a further command from God was issued after the Torah had been given (*Devarim* 5:27): "Let them return to their tent." (See also Rashi, s.v. "*Mino,*" and *Tosafot*, s.v. "*Mechdi.*")

31. *Devarim* 7:3–4.
32. **Kiddushin* 68b.
33. The Sages, in fact, agree that all intermarriage is prohibited, but they deduce it from a different text.
34. **Ketubot* 104a.

One minute before the conclusion of the Sabbath, anyone who kindles fire or chops wood has committed a capital offense; one minute later, these acts can be done with impunity.

Forty *se'ah* of water constitute a proper *mikveh;* one drop less and the *mikveh* has no power of ritual purification.

A ring worth one *prutah* passing from a man to a woman is a sufficient gift in a valid marriage ceremony.[35] If the ring is worth only a tenth of a *prutah* less, the ceremony has no legal effect.

The law, then, is strictly interpreted in all these cases; and it is to be strictly interpreted even if, as a result of strict interpretation, the obligation imposed by the law upon the individual becomes less onerous. It would be quite wrong, where the intention of the law is unknown, to invent an "intention" or "purpose" for a mitzvah and then object to a *Ha'aramah* on the grounds that it defeats the purpose one has invented.

To revert to the *Ha'aramah* of selling *chametz* to a non-Jew over Passover and purchasing it back after Passover. This, as has been said, is based upon the law that only *chametz* belonging to a Jew which had remained in existence over Passover is prohibited, but *chametz* belonging to a non-Jew which had remained in existence over Passover is permitted. If it were certain that the Torah had some objection to the very existence of *chametz* over Passover and confined its prohibition to *chametz* in the possession of Jews only because it legislates exclusively for Jews, then the *Ha'aramah* of selling *chametz* to a non-Jew and buying it back after Passover would be open to the objection that it destroys the spirit of the law. Since, however there is nothing to indicate that the Torah objects to *chametz* as such, it is absurd to invent a purpose for this law and then to protest that the selling of *chametz* defeats the purpose so invented.

This argument, however, must not be carried to too great a length. It must not be claimed that only the letter and not the spirit of the law is important.

35. Mishnah *Kiddushin* 1:1.

Loopholes Closed

Our purpose is to point out this difference between Torah law and other systems of law, and to make it clear that it is not always possible to think of the spirit of the law, in connection with Torah, in the same terms as are relevant to other systems.

In fact, the Sages expressly disapproved of a number of *Ha'aramot*, presumably because they appreciated that these devices did, in fact, destroy the spirit of the law in the cases considered.[36]

Maharatz Chajes[37] claims that the Sages did, in fact, consider *Ha'aramot* to be bad. However, according to Maharatz Chajes, they were prepared to allow *Ha'aramot* in cases where there was a danger that the laws concerned would otherwise be transgressed. The Sages thought it better that the people should make use of loopholes rather than transgress the law.

Presumably, then, where the Sages legislated to close loopholes, it was because they had no fear in the particular case that the law would be transgressed. For, as has been said, there were occasions when the Sages enacted laws to close loopholes.

For example, the Sages enacted a law which made corn liable for tithe, even where it had been winnowed by a non-Jew. This law was enacted when the Sages discovered that wealthy people transferred their corn to a non-Jew, so that it could be winnowed while in his ownership and so escape the incidence of tithe.[38]

They also enacted that an ox castrated by a non-Jew could not

36. For example, in the case of *heter iska*, which enables one to charge interest on a loan (contrary to *Vayikra* 25:35) by declaring it to be in the nature of a partnership venture. It has been said that although the *heter iska* can be used whatever the nature of the loan, it would be wrong to make use of it in order to take interest on a loan to a poor person. On the other hand, in connection with a commercial loan, why should a lender allow a large commercial enterprise to wax even bigger on his finance if he can charge interest through the medium of a *heter iska*?

37. *Darkei HaHoraah*, II.

38. **Menachot* 67a, and see Rashi, ad loc.

be retained by a Jew. This was because they found that owners were so arranging matters that their oxen should be castrated by a non-Jew.[39]

They also enacted legislation making unrolled dough liable for *challah*, because people were making use of a loophole in the law which made dough liable for *challah* only after it had been rolled.[40]

It is clear, therefore, that *Ha'aramot* were not always overlooked, nor were they always prohibited. The reaction of the Sages depended on the individual case, and whether or not in the judgment of the Sages the sanctity of the law concerned was imperiled.

SECTION III: THE SPIRIT OF HALACHAH – *LIFNIM MISHURAT HADIN* AND HIGHER LAW

We have argued that at times the spirit of *halachah* had to be forgone in order to safeguard the greater good of preserving some important Torah value. One such value, according to Rambam, is the principal that law has to be certain. Rambam writes:[41]

> The law does not take exceptional circumstances into account, it is not based on conditions which rarely occur. Whatever the law teaches, whether it be of an intellectual, moral or practical character, it is founded upon what the rule is and not what the exception is; it ignores the injury that might be caused to a single person through a certain maxim or a certain Divine precept.... The laws cannot, like medicine, vary according to the different conditions of people and times.

---

39. **Bava Metzia* 90a.
40. **Talmud Yerushalmi, Challah* 3:1.
41. **Moreh Nevuchim* 3:34. It must be noted that the "spirit of Halachah" was, in fact, treated with the greatest respect by Rambam. After explaining that there is an explicit command in the Torah not to allow a slave to do work on the Sabbath, Rambam writes: "Whoever understands the intention of the Torah and wants to follow it, will not only avoid making a slave do work which is prohibited to a Jew on the Sabbath, but in addition will not make a slave do even such work as is permitted to a Jew, such as any task involving great toil; or even wake a slave from his sleep." There is no specific law forbidding the waking of a slave from his sleep on the Sabbath, but Rambam relies on the spirit of Halachah for his legal ruling.

Here Rambam merely echoes the words of the Mishnah in *Masechet Ketubot*, which we have considered in some detail in the previous section,[42] and makes the point that law must be certain and cannot make exceptions presumably even when moral considerations or the spirit of law would dictate otherwise.

There are, however, a number of commandments in the Torah that are sometimes described as "higher law," or *Lifnim Mishurat haDin.* These laws are not expressed so as to impose a fixed and certain course of conduct or action, but are expressed in more general terms – "Be holy,"[43] or "...walk in the way of the good and keep the paths of the righteous,"[44] and impose an obligation which has the ultimate object of achieving fairness and ethical conduct.

Ramban[45] defines the mitzvah "be holy" (*kedoshim tihiyu*) in the following terms:

> The Torah has admonished us against immorality and forbidden food, but permitted sexual relations between a man and his wife, and the eating of certain meat and wine. If so, a man of desire could consider this to be a permission to be passionately addicted to sexual relations with his wife or many wives, and to be among the wine-bibbers, among gluttonous eaters of flesh, and to speak freely all profanities, since this prohibition has not been expressly mentioned in the Torah, and thus he will become a scoundrel who is nevertheless within the law of the Torah! Therefore, after having listed the matters that [God] prohibited altogether, the Torah followed them up by a general command that we practice moderation even in matters which are permitted.... It is with reference to these and similar matters that this general commandment "Be holy" is concerned....

42. See p. 121, and in footnote 34.
43. *Vayikra* 19:2.
44. *Mishlei* 2:20.
45. *Commenting on *Vayikra* 19:2.

These higher-law mitzvot have greater flexibility not only because the Torah expresses them in general terms, but also because they require general moral and ethical conduct, and must accordingly vary with each individual and the particular circumstances. This is made clear by the comments of R' Yeshayahu Horowitz (the Shlah):[46]

> Each man has his own law under this principle...if the nature of all men were the same and all times were the same, then [under the principle *kedoshim tihiyu*] the Torah would have written, "eat the following measure of food..." and anything in excess would be forbidden. The same would apply in connection with relations with one's wife and in connection with talk and thought. However, it is impossible to say this [except to make a general law – *kedoshim tihiyu*] the explanation of which is: be holy in connection with that which is excessive for you. This means, whatever you feel is excessive, according to the circumstances and according to your nature, is forbidden to you by the Torah.[47]

The manner in which *Lifnim Mishurat haDin* law is applied in practice is well illustrated by a case which came before Rav in his capacity as a judge and is reported in the Talmud[48] as follows:

---

46. *Shnei Luchot HaBrit, Torah sheBichtav, Kedoshim,* p. 58b.

47. There are similar comments by the *Maggid Mishneh (in Rambam's *Hilchot Shechenim* 14:5), who writes: *Kedoshim tihiyu* – "Be holy," meaning, as the Rabbis said, sanctify yourself with respect to that which is permitted to you, not to pursue your lust. Likewise, it is said, "And you shall do the right and the good," meaning that one's interpersonal conduct should be good and just. With regard to all this, it would not have been right to demand details, for the Torah's commands apply to all periods and under all circumstances, whereas man's character and his behavior vary with the time and the individual.

    See also *Yismach Moshe* (Berlin: Pardes, 1928), p. 20: "The command 'Be holy' even in matters which are permitted can be performed in one of two ways – either by refraining from excessive indulgence, or, on the contrary, by indulging excessively in the permitted in order not to be tempted to indulge in the forbidden. It all depends on the person and the time.

48. **Bava Metzia* 83a.

> Certain porters broke barrels of wine belonging to Rabbah bar bar Chanah (or, Rabbah the son of Rav Huna). He thereupon retained their clothes as a lien for the damage they had caused. They came and complained to Rav. He said to Rabbah bar bar Chanah, "Return their clothes!"
>
> "Is this the *din?"* he asked.
>
> "Yes," Rav answered. "[The verse states:] 'that you may walk in the way of good men.'"
>
> He returned their clothes.
>
> The porters then said, "We are poor, and have worked all day; we are hungry, and we have nothing."
>
> Rav said to Rabbah bar bar Chanah, "Pay them their wage." He again asked, "Is this the *din?*
>
> "Yes," answered Rav. "[The verse continues:] '...and keep the path of the righteous.'"

Although Rav said, "Yes, this is the *din*," according to the commentators[49] this ruling, unlike ordinary *halachah*, applies only to important personalities and wealthy individuals in their dealings with the general public.

The regular *halachah* says, "Do not give preference to a poor man in law." The *Lifnim Mishurat haDin* says, in certain circumstances:[50]

---

49. *Mordechai, Bava Metzia* 24b and *Aruch HaShulchan* 304:11; *Shitah Mekubetzet,* ad loc., "Rabbi Yonatan: We force only an important man to pay."

   Whether *Lifnim Mishurat haDin* can be enforced by a *bet din* is subject to a dispute among the *poskim*. See *Sdei Chemed* 3, p. 282, s.v. "*Middat Sdom*" (e.g. where a person demands payment for a benefit which costs the provider nothing to supply). See also *Kiddushin* 32a; *Shulchan Aruch, Yoreh De'ah* 240.

   In any event, *Lifnim Mishurat haDin* is not to be treated lightly. Jerusalem was destroyed because the inhabitants insisted on the strict *din* rather than *Lifnim Mishurat haDin* (see *Bava Metzia* 30b).

   See also A. Lichtenstein in *Encounter* (Jerusalem, 1989), p. 76; and my essay, "Morality and Halachah," in the same book, p. 102, for a detailed treatment of "higher law" and *Lifnim Mishurat haDin.*

50. It is clear from the text that there was no strict legal obligation on Rav to return the clothes and pay the wages to the porter. There is a dispute among the commentators as to why no such obligation arises. Some suggest the porters were negligent. The problem then arises: Why was there no moral obligation on Rav to pay? It cannot

"We will oblige him to pay if he can afford to pay" and "if the worker is needy and helpless." The spirit, rather than the letter, of the law dictates that Rabbah bar bar Chanah be forced to pay because he was wealthy and the workers were destitute. The obligation to pay was created by the moral Torah principle of compassion and not by the strict *halachah.* The Halachah lays down the minimum standard with which every Jew must comply, be he rich or poor, high or low. *Lifnim Mishurat haDin* aspires to the ideal and to perfection.

The path of the righteous does not recognize the limitations of a rigid law, but seeks a law that will vary with the individual and the circumstances, in pursuit of equality and justice. Man must aspire to "be holy" and "walk in the way of good men." He must strive after the spirit of the higher law – and not be satisfied with serving the body of the law without its soul.

be solely because he was rich and they were poor. One suggestion is that there was insufficient evidence of their negligence. For a detailed discussion, see Rashi, ad loc., Meiri, *Shitah Mekubetzet, Igrot Moshe, Choshen Mishpat* 1:60.

Hebrew Sources

SECTION I

Ha'aramot Which Serve as a Reminder of the Law

5. Shabbat 117b

אותו ואת בנו שנפלו לבור רבי אליעזר אומר מעלה את הראשון על מנת לשוחטו והשני עושה לו פרנסה במקומו בשביל שלא ימות. רבי יהושע אומר מעלין את הראשון על מנת לשוחטו ואינו שוחטו, ומערים ומעלה את השני רצה זה שוחט רצה זה שוחט.

11. Moed Katan 19a

ת"ר כותב אדם תפילין ומזוזות לעצמו, וטווה על יריכו תכלת לציציתו ולאחרים בטובה דברי רבי מאיר, ר' יהודה אומר מערים ומוכר את שלו וחוזר וכותב לעצמו. ר' יוסי אומר כותב ומוכר כדרכו כדי פרנסתו.

16. Gittin 36a

תנן התם פרוסבול אינו משמט, זה אחד מן הדברים שהתקין הלל הזקן, שראה את העם שנמנעו מלהלוות זה את זה, ועברו על מה שכתוב בתורה "השמר לך פן יהיה דבר עם לבבך בליעל וגו'" (דברים ט"ז) עמד והתקין פרוסבול. וזה הוא גופו של פרוסבול מוסרני לכם פלוני דיינין שבמקום פלוני שכל חוב שיש לי אצל פלוני שאגבנו כל זמן שארצה, והדיינים חותמים למטה או העדים.

ומי איכא מידי דמדאורייתא משמטא שביעית והתקין הלל דלא משמטא? אמר אביי בשביעית בזמן הזה ורבי היא. (והלל כרבי סבירה ליה דאמר שביעית להשמטת מלוה בזמן הזה דרבנן הוא - רש"י). רבא אמר הפקר ב"ד היה הפקר.

SECTION II

Ha'aramot Which Conform with the Letter of the Law

21. Berachot 31a

מערים אדם על תבואתו ומכניסה במוץ שלה כדי שתהא בהמתו אוכלת ופטורה מן המעשר.

22. Mishnah Ma'aser Sheni 4:4

מערימין על מעשר שני, כיצד? אומר אדם לבנו ולבתו הגדולים, לעבדו ושפחתו העברים, "הילך מעות אלה ופדה לך מעשה שני זה". אבל לא יאמר כן לבנו ולבתו הקטנים ועבדו ולשפחתו הכנענים מפי שידן כידו.

24. Mishnah Nedarim 5:6

המודר הנאה מחבירו. ואין לו מה יאכל, נותנו לאחר לשום מתנה והלה מותר בה.

27. Tosefta, Pesachim 2:6

ישראל ונכרי, שהיו באין בספינה וחמץ ביד ישראל הרי זה מוכרו לנכרי ונותנו במתנה וחוזר ולוקח ממנו לאחר הפסח. ובלבד שיתנו לו במתנה גמורה.

The Law and its Reason or Purpose

28. Megillah 25a

מתני': האומר... על קן ציפור יגיעו רחמיך... משתקין אותו: גמ': מ"ט...מפני שעושה מדותיו של הקב"ה רחמים ואינן אלא גזירות.

32. Kiddushin 66b and 68b

מתני': וכל מי שאין לה לא עליו ולא על אחרים קידושין הולד כמותה ואיזה זה ולד שפחה ונכרית:

גמ': נכרית מנלן? אמר קרא "לא תתחתן בם" (דברים ז'). אשכחנא דלא תפסי בה קידושי ולדה כמותה מנלן? אמר א"ר יוחנן משום ר"ש בן יוחי דאמר קרא "כי יסיר את בנך מאחרי" בנך הבא מישראלית קרוי בנך ואין בנך הבא מן העובדת כוכבים קרוי בנך אלא בנה.... ההוא בשבעה גוים כתיב! שאר אומות מנלן? א"ק "כי יסיר את בנך" לרבות כל המסירים. הניחא לר"ש דדריש טעמא דקרא אלא לרבנן מ"ט?

The Law is Strictly Interpreted

34. Ketubot 104a

מתני׳... וחכ״א כל זמן שהיא בבית בעלה גובה כתובתה לעולם כל זמן שהיא בבית אביה גובה כתובתה עד עשרים וחמש שנים.

גמ׳: אמר ליה אביי לרב יוסף אתאי קודם שקיעת החמה גובה כתובתה, לאחר שקיעת החמה לא גביא, בהיא פורתא אחילתא? א״ל אין, כל מדת חכמים כן היא בארבעים סאה טובל בארבעים סאה חסר קורטוב אינו יכול לטבול בהן.

Loopholes Which Were Closed

38. Menachot 67a

והא האי תנא דאמר מירוח העכו״ם אינו פוטר, גלגול העכו״ם פוטר? מדרבנן, גזירה משום בעלי כיסים. (שיש להם קרקעות הרבה וחסים על רוב מעשרות ויקנוהו לעכו״ם וימריחום עכו״ם ומפקע ליה ממעשר - רש״י).

39. Bava Metzia 90a

ת״ש דשלחו ליה לאבוה דשמואל הלין תורי דגנבין ארמאי ומגנחין יתהון (ומסרסין אותם ואח״כ מחזירין לבעלים ומאהבת בעליו ישראל גונבו הנכרי - רש״י) מהו? שלח להו הערמה אתעביד בהו אערימו עלייהו ויזדבנון.

40. Talmud Yerushalmi, Challah 3:1

אוכלין עראי מן העיסה עד שתגלגל.

אמר ר׳ חגיי לא שנו אלא עראי אבל קבע אסור. מפני שהוא מערים לפוטרה מן החלה.

SECTION III

Law Must Be Certain

41. Rambam, Moreh Nevuchim 3:34

ממה שאתה צריך לדעת עוד, כי אין התורה מביטה על הבודד, ולא יהיה הצווי כפי הדבר המועט, אלא כל מה שרצוי להשיגו, השקפה או מדה או מעשה מועיל, אין מביטים בו אלא לדברים שהם הרוב, ואין שמים לב לדבר מועט האירוע, ולא לנזק

שיהיה ליחיד מבני אדם בגלל אותה הגזרה וההנהגה התורתית, כי התורה היא דבר אלהי, ויש לך ללמוד מן הדברים הטבעיים אשר אותם התועליות הכלליות המצויות בהן, יש בכללן ומתחייב מהן נזקים אישיים. כמו שנתבאר בדברנו ודברי זולתנו. ועל פי הבחנה זו, כך אל תתפלא שאין מטרות התורה מתקיימים בכל אחד ואחד, אלא מתחייב בהחלט שימצאו אנשים שאין אותו הניהול התורתי מביא להם שלמות, כי הצורות הטבעיות המיניות לא יושג כל מה שמתחייב מהן בכל אחד ואחד, כי הכל מאלוה אחד ופועל אחד, נתנו מרועה אחד, והפך זה נמנע, וכבר בארנו כי לנמנע טבע קבוע לא ישתנה לעולם. ועוד על פי הבחנה זו לא יתכן שיהו המצות נרשמות כפי שנויי מצבי בני אדם והזמנים, כמו הרכבת התרופה, שמיוחדת הרכבה לכל אדם כפי מזגו באותה העת, אלא ראוי שתהא ההנהגה התורתית מוחלטת כללית לכל, ואף על פי שיהא זה חיובי ביחס לאנשים, וביחס לאחרים אינו חיובי כי אלו היו לפי היחידים יהיה הפסד לכל, ונתת דבריך לשיעורין. ומפני זה אין ראוי שיוגבלו הדברים המכוונים מטרה ראשונה שבתורה, לא בזמן ולא במקום, אלא יהיו הדינים החלטיים באופן כללי, כמו שאמר יתעלה הקהל חקה אחת לכם, אלא מכוון בהם התועליות הכלליות שהן על הרוב כמו שבארנו.

ואחר שהקדמתי הקדמות הללו אחל לבאר את אשר נתכוונתי לבאר.

Higher Law

45. Ramban, Vayikra 19:2

כי התורה הזהירה בעריות ובמאכלים האסורים והתירה הביאה איש באשתו ואכילת הבשר והיין א״כ ימצא בעל התאוה מקום להיות שטוף בזמת אשתו או נשיו הרבות ולהיות בסובאי יין ובזוללי בשר למו וידבר כרצונו בכל הנבלות שלא הוזכר איסור זה בתורה והנה יהיה נבל ברשות התורה לפיכך בא הכתוב אחרי שפרט האיסורים שאסר אותם לגמרי וצוה בדבר כללי שנהיה פרושים מן המותרות...

47. Maggid Mishneh in Rambam's Hilchot Shechenim 14:5

באמירת קדושים תהיו והכוונה כמו שאמרו ז״ל קדש עצמך במותר לך שלא יהא שטוף אחר התאוות וכן אמרה ועשית הישר והטוב והכוונה שיתנהג בהנהגה טובה וישרה עם בני אדם ולא היה מן ראוי בכל זה לצוות פרטים לפי שמצות התורה הם בכל עת ובכל זמן ובכל ענין ובהכרח חייב לעשות כן ומדות האדם והנהגתו מתחלפת לפי הזמן והאישים.

48. Bava Metzia 83a

רבה בר בר חנן תברו ליה הנהו שקולאי חביתא דחמרא שקל לגלימייהו אתו אמרו

לרב אמר ליה הב להו גלימייהו אמר ליה דינא הכי אמר ליה אין למען תלך בדרך טובים יהיב להו גלימייהו אמרו ליה עניי אנן וטרחינן כולה יומא וכפינן ולית לן מידי א"ל זיל הב אגרייהו א"ל דינא הכי אמר ליה אין וארחות צדיקים תשמר.

Chapter 8

The Mishnah of the Sages

INTRODUCTION[1]

No discussion of the contribution made by the Sages to the Oral Law is complete without a reference to their work in connection with the Mishnah. The Mishnah is the basis of the Oral Law which is known to us, and its formulation was entirely the work of the Sages. There is no suggestion that the text of the Mishnah is of Divine origin. What, in fact, is its origin?[(א)] In this chapter, we will discuss various views regarding the origin and purpose of the Mishnaic arrangement.

Midrashic and Mishnaic Styles Distinguished

The Mishnah normally comprises a simple statement of the law, or of a difference of Rabbinic opinion concerning the law, and it does not make any reference to the Scripture. For example, the Mishnah[2] states: "Fifteen women render their co-wives...free from Levirate marriage." This statement is in the Mishnaic style, and does not adduce any Scriptural

1. It may be of assistance to the reader to refer also to the Introduction to this book, p. xxiii, paragraphs 2 and 3.
2. Mishnah *Yevamot* 1:1.

proof. Occasionally, a *mishnah* will refer to the Scriptural passage on which it is based,[3] it is then said to be in Midrashic style. The *Sifra* and *Sifrei* are entirely in Midrashic style; the Mishnah, on the other hand, as the name suggests is almost entirely in Mishnaic style.

Which Came First?

In a passage contained in his famous letter addressed to the community at Kairawan, Rav Sherira Gaon, tenth-century head of the Academy in Pumbedita, remarks: "*Sifra* and *Sifrei* are *drash* on the Scripture...and in the early times, in the days of the Second Temple, in the days of the early masters, this was the method of learning."[4] From this statement it appears that the Midrashic style of the *Sifra* and *Sifrei* preceded the Mishnaic style, and it has been thought accordingly that the origin of the Mishnah is to be found in Midrashic statements of law.[5] For example, the Mishnah which we have quoted may have originated from a Midrashic text in the following form: "Fifteen women render their co-wives...free from Levirate marriage...as it is written:[6] 'Neither shall you take a wife to her sister as her rival.'" Later the Midrashic statement of *halachah* was stripped of its scriptural proof and became known as a *mishnah*. Those who write about this change of style claim that the change took place at about the time when the *Tanna'im* embarked upon the first arrangement of the Mishnah. This leads us to the first problem to be discussed in this chapter: When did the first arrangement of the Mishnah take place?

SECTION I: THE FIRST MISHNAH ARRANGEMENT

Various passages of the Talmud and of other early writings have been said to provide a clue to the period when the first arrangement of the Mishnah took place, and it may be rewarding to examine some of these

3. For instance, Mishnah *Nega'im* 12:5 et seq.; Mishnah *Sotah* 8:1-2; Mishnah *Yevamot* 12:6; Mishnah *Sanhedrin* 1:4 et seq., 2:4, 4:5, 6:2 et seq.
4. **Iggeret Rav Sherira Gaon*, A. Hyman, ed. (London, 1910; Jerusalem, 1967), p. 39.
5. See, for instance, Rav D.Z. Hoffman, *Die Erste Mischna.*
6. *Vayikra* 18:18.

passages in detail. We shall consider the evidence produced in support of five different periods (not taken in chronological order).

The Time of Yavneh

Firstly, we turn to the Tosefta in *Eduyot.*[7] This states that when the Sages entered *Kerem b'Yavneh* they said, "A time will come when a man will seek a matter from the words of the Torah and not find it, from the words of the scribes and not find it... No one thing of the Torah will be like the other," and as a result they embarked upon an arrangement of the *mishnayot* of Hillel and Shammai.

It has been said[8] that this passage indicates the concern the Sages felt for the future of the Oral Law in the absence of any systematic arrangement of *mishnayot.* It follows from this that at the time of Yavneh, there was no such arrangement.

It also follows that *Masechet Eduyot,* which was then produced, was the beginning of the first collection of *mishnayot.*

It is, however, questionable whether this is the correct interpretation of the Tosefta.[9] Moreover, if the Sages were, in fact, concerned about the need for a *mishnah* arrangement they would not have sought the remedy in an arrangement like *Masechet Eduyot,* which classifies *mishnayot* according to the *Tanna'im* whose statements are recorded. Such a classification would not have been sensible at a time when most *mishnayot* were anonymous.

The Time of R. Akiva

It is necessary to consider next a dictum in *Masechet Sanhedrin:*[10] "Whenever an anonymous opinion is stated in the Mishnah it is that of R. Meir, in the Tosefta that of R. Nechemiah, in the *Sifra* that of R. Yehudah, and in the *Sifrei* that of R. Shimon – and they all follow R. Akiva."[(ב)]

---

7. *Tosefta, *Eduyot* 1:1.
8. Chanoch Albeck, *Mavo LaMishnah* (Jerusalem, 1959), p. 82.
9. See pp. 145 and 155.
10. **Sanhedrin* 86a.

On the basis of this dictum, it has been suggested[11] that R. Akiva is responsible for the first *mishnah* arrangement, that he was the first to organize *halachot* in a logical manner, and that the other *Tanna'im* who are said to "follow R. Akiva" followed his example in their collection of *halachot*. It will be realized that this passage from *Masechet Sanhedrin* is capable of more than one interpretation.[12] Moreover, the same may be said of an Aggadic passage, which had similarly been claimed to refer to R. Akiva's work of arranging *mishnayot*.[13]

The *Aggadah* concerned likens R. Akiva "to a worker who takes his basket and goes out to find corn and collects it in his basket. He finds oat and puts it in, spelt and puts it in, and so on. When he enters his house, he sorts out the wheat separately and the spelt separately."[14(2)]

The Time of Bet Shammai and Bet Hillel

A much earlier period for the first arrangement of the Mishnah is suggested by a Responsa in *Shaarei Teshuvah*.[15] There we read as follows:

> You should know that from the days of Moshe Rabbenu to Hillel haZaken there were six hundred orders of the Mishnah[16] that were given by God to Moshe at Sinai. From Hillel onwards the world became impoverished and diminished and the glory of the Torah weakened, and from Hillel and Shammai they produced no more than six orders.

It has been said[17] on the basis of this text that the Mishnah was first arranged at the time of Bet Hillel and Bet Shammai. Combining this with the statement of Rav Sherira Gaon[18] that at about that time *halachot*

---

11. Zechariah Frankel, *Darkei HaMishnah* (Tel Aviv, 1959), p. 15.
12. See infra p. 141–142.
13. Zechariah Frankel, op. cit., p. 221.
14. *Avot D'Rabbi Natan* 18:1.
15. **Shaarei Teshuvah* 1:20.
16. See also *Chagigah* 14a for reference to six hundred orders of the Mishnah.
17. Rav D.Z. Hoffman, op. cit.
18. See p. 136.

ceased to be presented in Midrashic style, the conclusion is reached that the arrangement of the Mishnah and the changing of the form of halachic texts were really part and parcel of the same venture undertaken in the time of Bet Shammai and Bet Hillel.

The Time of the Anshei Knesset haGedolah

There is, however, one view which suggests an even earlier period for the first *mishnah* arrangement. It is not based on any external evidence, but on the text of the Mishnah itself. This is the view of R' I.I. Halevy,[19] who looks to the period of the *Anshei Knesset haGedolah* for the first complete *mishnah* arrangement.

He argues as follows: All disputes between *Tanna'im* that are reported in the Mishnah concern some point arising out of a *principle* that has been stated either in the same or in a previous *mishnah*. The *Tanna'im* never dispute or refute this principle but they invariably argue about its application in detail only. It follows that the statement of principle preceded the argument of the *Tanna'im* in point of time. This statement of principle which may be called *"yesod haMishnah"* is part of an original *mishnah* collection which covers all the principles of the Oral Law.[20]

---

19. **Dorot HaRishonim* 1:3, p. 206.

20. It will be useful to analyze two *mishnayot* in accordance with R' Halevy's theory. (In the following two *mishnayot*, the *yesod haMishnah* is presented in italics.)

Mishnah I: "*If a corpse lay in a room to which there are many entrances, they are all unclean... If there was intention to take the corpse out through one of the entrances, this affords protection to all other entrances.* Bet Shammai says the intention must have been formed before the death occurred, Bet Hillel says it is enough if the intention was formed after the death" (Mishnah *Ohalot* 7:3).

The *yesod* here lays down the undisputed principle: the argument centers around the word "intention" in that principle – i.e. at what point in time must the *intention* have been present?

Mishnah II: "*A woman is acquired by three ways...by money, by writ or by intercourse.* By money, Bet Shammai says by a *dinar*...and Bet Hillel says by a *prutah*" (Mishnah *Kiddushin* 1:1).

Again the *yesod* lays down the general principle and the argument concerns the amount of "money."

Chanoch Albeck criticizes R' Halevy for failing to distinguish between an old law and an old Mishnah text. He says that the fact that Bet Shammai and Bet Hillel

There are no disputes concerning these principles, as distinct from their application in detail. Since there are no disputes, we must conclude that the *yesod haMishnah* dates back to the period of the *Anshei Knesset haGedolah* when there was a Sanhedrin and "there were no disputes in Israel." The Sanhedrin, of course, continued to function down to the time of Hillel and Shammai, but after the period of the *Anshei Knesset haGedolah* conditions in the land were so unsettled that no halachic work of any major importance could have been undertaken.

If this idea of *yesod haMishnah* is accepted, then it will be discovered that frequently the *yesod haMishnah* is in Mishnaic style and the disputes which are later additions to it are in *Midrashic* style.[21] This contradicts the findings previously discussed – that the Midrashic style

---

and later *Tanna'im* often argue concerning details of a principle set out in the *yesod haMishnah* does not prove that the text of the *yesod* is of early origin. It merely shows that the principle of law contained in the *yesod*, i.e. the subject matter of the *mishnayot*, is of long standing.

According to Albeck, *mishnah* I shows merely that the extent to which a corpse spreads its uncleanness was well established long before the time of Bet Shammai and Bet Hillel, and *mishnah* II shows the same regarding the requirement of money in a marriage contract. There is, however, no proof that these principles existed in the form of an established *mishnah* text. Bet Hillel and Bet Shammai did not have before them a general arrangement of the Mishnah, but a number of long-standing statements of law which were well established in their time, and which had not yet assumed a settled text. These laws might be expressed variously by the different schools of the time: for example, while some taught "by three ways a woman is acquired...," others taught "a man acquires a woman by…," and yet others "a contract of marriage is concluded by a man giving to a woman…," Chanoch Albeck, op. cit., pp. 65 and 82.

Rabbi J.J. Weinberg (*Samuel Mirsky Jubilee Volume* [New York, 1958]), however, comes to R' Halevy's support. He feels that a close textual analysis shows that the controversies between Bet Shammai and Bet Hillel in the cases referred to, concern not merely principles of law, but also the expression of those principles in a given text. He points out that in *mishnah* II, the repetition of the words "by money" as an introduction to the controversy indicates that Bet Shammai and Bet Hillel were defining a term in a text, and in *mishnah* I, the same is true of the word "intention."

21. The following examples will illustrate this argument. (What R' Halevy calls the *yesod haMishnah* is in italics.)

"If a man ate Terumah in error, he must pay its value plus one-fifth" (Mishnah *Terumot* 6:1).

"R. Eliezer says: 'Restitution may be made for one kind instead of another kind'... R. Akiva says: 'Restitution may be made only for the like kind.' R. Eliezer says:

preceded the Mishnaic. R. Halevy[22] accordingly, is of the view that both styles together had long been in use, sometimes the one and sometimes the other.

The Time of R. Yehudah haNasi

Having discussed a view which puts the date of the first Mishnah arrangement as far back as possible, it is proposed to conclude with a view which goes to the other extreme and puts the late forward as far as possible. In this connection, we must again refer to the famous letter of Rav Sherira Gaon where the problem under discussion is specifically raised.

According to Rav Sherira Gaon, before the time of R. Yehudah haNasi they "did not have a generally accepted arrangement of the Mishnah in a uniform style and language. Although all the Sages were agreed on the substance of the oral tradition, every one of them taught his pupils in whatever order or style he preferred."[23]

There were different schools which taught identical principles, but they were taught in a variety of styles. R. Yehudah was the first to arrange the Mishnah. He did this by taking *mishnayot* from the various

---

"'and he shall give to the priests the holy things" (*Vayikra* 22:14), namely whatever is fit to be holy.' But R. Akiva says: 'The same kind of holy thing as he has eaten" (Mishnah *Terumot* 6:6).

"*What counts as a defective cluster of grapes (olelot)? Any cluster that lacks both shoulders and pendant*" (Mishnah *Pe'ah* 7:4).

"If a vineyard has only defective clusters, R. Elazar says: 'They belong to the householder.' R. Akiva says: 'They belong to the poor.' R. Eliezer says: "'When you gather the grapes of your vineyard you shall not take defective clusters" (*Devarim* 24:21). If there is no grape gathering, how can there be defective clusters?' R. Akiva said to him: "'And from your vineyard you shall not take defective clusters'" (*Vayikra* 19:10) even if they are all defective clusters" (Mishnah *Pe'ah* 7:7).

22. *Op. cit. 1:5, p. 543 et seq. R' Halevy also points out that according to *Yevamot* 72b, R. Yochanan had never studied the *Sifrei*. If the entire Mishnah is based on Midrashic *halachot*, it is impossible that R. Yochanan should have been ignorant of the most important *Midrash Halachah*.

23. *Op. cit., p. 28 et seq.

schools – showing special preference for those which once came from the school of R. Meir[24] – and arranging them in a logical order.[25]

SECTION II: THE PURPOSE OF THE MISHNAIC ARRANGEMENT

A Change in Style to Clarify the Law

In arranging the Mishnah, the endeavor of the Sages was not only the *classification* of the material of the Oral Law but also, as we shall try to show, the *clarification* of the law as it then stood.[ד] We would even suggest that the change which they made from the Midrashic to the Mishnaic style was motivated by their endeavor to clarify the laws.[ה] Firstly, however we shall mention three widely accepted theories which have been put forward to account for this change in style.

Three Theories

1. The Mishnaic style was preferred, because it was easier to memorize. This would be an important consideration at a time when it was not permitted to reduce the Oral Law to writing.
2. With the increase of Rabbinic legislation, which does not rely on Scriptural proof, the Midrashic style was no longer suitable.
3. The Midrashic style was abandoned because it followed the arrangement of the law in the Pentateuch, and as the Pentateuch deals with different aspects of the identical topic in various places it was not possible to classify *halachot* in order of subject matter while following the Midrashic manner of study.

---

24. This is the usual interpretation of the passage from the Talmud, *Sanhedrin* 86a, quoted on p. 137. Not all anonymous *mishnayot* follow R. Meir: See *Ketubot* 71a, *Yevamot* 111b, *Bava Batra* 65b. The Mishnah of R. Shimon Ish haMitzpeh was chosen for *Masechet Yoma* (see *Yoma* 14b); that of R. Eliezer ben Yaakov for *Masechet Middot* (see *Yoma* 16a); and that of R. Yose for *Masechet Eruvin* and *Masechet Ohalot* (see *Eruvin* 79a).
25. Those *mishnayot* that were not included in the collection are known as *baraitot*, "outside" texts.

A New Theory

It may be, however, that the truth lies elsewhere: that the Sages endeavored at the time of classification of the law also to achieve clarification of *halachah* and that the Midrashic style was abandoned because it lacked the necessary authority. When a *halachah* is stated to be derived from a Scriptural passage, it is open to the argument that the passage concerned has been misinterpreted. The Mishnaic style, on the other hand, bears the hallmark of finality, and the *halachah* is stated beyond all argument.[26]

Two Eras of Clarification

The endeavor of the Sages to clarify the Oral Law at the same time as they arranged it systematically, is borne out by the two major arrangements of the Mishnah about which one can write with certainty.

Although it has been seen that there is no general agreement on the question when the *first* arrangement of the Mishnah took place, it is beyond dispute that there was an arrangement of some *mishnayot* at Yavneh and again at the time of R. Yehudah haNasi.

Even Rav Sherira Gaon, who declares that R. Yehudah haNasi was the first "to arrange the Halachah so that the Rabbis should cite the law in a uniform language and style,"[27] refers to the arrangement of *Masechet Eduyot* which took place in Yavneh generations earlier.[28]

---

26. This may explain R' Halevy's findings that the *yesod haMishnah* is frequently in Mishnaic style, whereas the argument of later *Tanna'im* which follows is in Midrashic style. The Mishnaic passage represents a statement of established law which had accordingly been cast in Mishnaic style, whereas the Midrashic passage, being more recent in origin, had not yet undergone the process of change. *See Avodah Zarah* 35a that the Sages of Eretz Yisrael never disclosed their reason at the time that they promulgated a *Gezerah*, because the *Gezerah* was more respected when its reason was not stated." (ז)

27. Op. cit., p. 32.

28. Rav Sherira Gaon also refers to *Masechet Uktzin* which was known in the time of R. Shimon ben Gamliel (see *Horiyot* 13b). *Masechet Kelim* was known to R. Yose who

Yavneh

It will be shown in this chapter that both the generation of Yavneh and that of R. Yehudah haNasi had made it their concern to see that the Halachah should be clearly stated and should speak with a single voice. First, let us deal with three indications that at the time of Yavneh the Sages endeavored to clarify the law.

Masechet Eduyot

Masechet Eduyot speaks for the efforts made by the Sages at Yavneh to clarify the law. It comprises, as its name suggests, the "evidence" of the scholars regarding traditional rulings of law. It also clarifies the law regarding the many disputes between Bet Shammai and Bet Hillel. According to the *Talmud Yerushalmi*, Yavneh was the place where a *Bat Kol* announced[29] that the rulings of both Bet Shammai and Bet Hillel were "the words of the living God" but that the rulings of Bet Hillel were law.[30]

The Struggle With R. Eliezer

R. Gamliel, the *Nasi* of that period, showed his determination to assert a single unified halachic authority. He even excommunicated his colleague R. Eliezer when the latter refused to bow to the halachic ruling of the majority of Sages. R. Eliezer's ruling had the support of a *Bat Kol.*[31] Nevertheless, he was told that the "Torah was not in Heaven" and the view of the majority of Sages must prevail. R. Gamliel explained his action in the following prayer: "Sovereign of the universe! You know full well that I have not acted for my honor nor for the honor of my parent's house, but for Yours, so that strife may not multiply in Israel."

---

knew how the *masechet* had been arranged, hence his statement (Mishnah *Kelim* 30:4): "Blessed are You, O *Kelim*, for you entered in uncleanness but went forth in cleanness." See *Sefer Kritut*.

29. *Talmud Yerushalmi, Yevamot* 1:6: "The *Bat Kol* came at Yavneh."
30. *Eruvin* 13b.
31. **Bava Metzia* 59b.

The Struggle With R. Yehoshua

R. Gamliel of Yavneh was determined that strife might not multiply in Israel, and that a unified halachic authority should declare the law. When R. Yehoshua contradicted his authority on several occasions, R. Gamliel treated him with such severity that the people revolted on behalf of R. Yehoshua, and R. Gamliel had to step down from his high office.[32]

Yavneh was a time of comparative calm in the midst of political upheavals in the land, and the Sages felt that they must grasp the opportunity to establish the authority of the Halachah. The urge to put an end to strife and to establish universally accepted halachic rulings arose out of the concern of the Sages expressed in the Tosefta which has been cited earlier.[33] This Tosefta speaks of the fear the Sages had expressed at Yavneh that a time might come when a man would seek a clear ruling of *halachah* without success. It has been seen that the concern of the Sages was attributed to the lack of a systematic arrangement of *halachah*. It is more likely, however, what really worried the Sages was the uncertainty of the law caused by conflicting authority, because there would be no resemblance between the words of the Torah as expressed by Bet Shammai and the words of the Torah as expressed by Bet Hillel.

In organizing the material of the Oral Law at Yavneh, the Sages, therefore, were mindful not only of the need to produce a more convenient reference to the Oral Law, but also of the call for a more definite statement of the law as it stood.

R. Yehudah haNasi

The redaction of the Mishnah by R. Yehudah haNasi presents a similar pattern of classification and clarification. It has been said that "his great achievement in the days of finalizing the Mishnah was that of deciding controversies which had remained unresolved since the days of Yavneh and turning such decisions into anonymous *mishnayot*."[34] In

32. *Berachot* 27b.
33. See p. 137, footnote 7.
34. The following points should be made clear regarding the "anonymous *mishnah*"

this undertaking, R. Yehudah haNasi was assisted by the members of his *Bet Din.*[35]

The Anonymous Mishnah

These anonymous *mishnayot* clarified the law on halachic problems which had been the subject of disputes. True that a law contained in an anonymous *mishnah* may appear elsewhere in the *mishnah* arrangement as still subject to a dispute. But there are rules for recognizing the *halachah* in such a case. Before these rules can be understood, something has to be said about the *mishnah* arrangement in general.

The Arrangement of Mishnayot

Whether the arrangement by R. Yehudah haNasi is identical with that which is found in our present-day Mishnah is open to question. The Six Orders (*Sedarim*), as arranged at present, follow this sequence:

1. *Zera'im* (dealing mainly with the laws of the Land of Israel and its fruit)
2. *Mo'ed* (laws of the Sabbath and Festivals)

(*stam mishnah*).

a. Anonymous *mishnayot* are frequently the result of R. Yehudah haNasi's work. See *Rosh Hashanah* 7b, *Chullin* 84a. The Talmud occasionally refers to anonymous *mishnayot* as "here Rebbi learned." See **Gittin* 29a.

b. Not all anonymous *mishnayot* are the result of Rebbi's work of deciding *halachot.* Many *mishnayot* had always been anonymous, because the law they state was never subject to any controversy.

c. Sometimes, instead of presenting a decision of halachah as an anonymous mishnah, Rebbi presents it as the view of "the Sages."

d. That the Halachah follows the anonymous mishnayot is stated by R. Yochanan (see *Shabbat* 46a), but see a general discussion of this proposition by S.K. Mirsky in The Leo Jung Jubilee Volume (New York), p. 155 et seq.

35. Mishnah *Ohalot* 18:9 and Mishnah *Gittin* 5:6. There are a number of instances in which Rebbi's view was defeated by a vote taken in the *Bet Din.* Consequently, there are anonymous *mishnayot* which carry the rider that R. Yehudah took a different view of the law.

3. *Nashim* (marriage and divorce)
4. *Nezikin* (torts)
5. *Kodashim* (laws relating to the Temple, its vessels and the sacrifices)
6. *Taharot* (laws of ritual purity)

It is, however, by no means certain that this is the arrangement which R. Yehudah haNasi followed. While this arrangement is referred to in the Talmud,[36] the Midrash[37] knew of a different sequence of the order of the Mishnah.

The origin of the sequence of *masechtot* within each *seder* is similarly in doubt. While the Talmud provides an explanation why the *sedarim* follow each other in the particular order mentioned,[38] the commentators have great difficulty in finding a rational explanation for the sequence in which the *masechtot* follow one another. In some respects, our present arrangement is quite extraordinary; there are such anomalies as the tractate dealing with divorce preceding that dealing with the laws of marriage.[39] It has been said[40] that the *masechtot* were arranged in order of size, with those having a greater number of chapters preceding those with lesser numbers.[41] However, this explanation is not completely satisfactory; *Seder Zera'im* does not follow that pattern.

---

36. R. Shimon ben Lakish, *Shabbat* 31a.
37. *Yalkut Tehillim* 9; the order there is *Nashim, Zera'im, Taharot, Moed, Kodashim* and *Nezikin.*
38. It is said to follow *Yeshayahu* 33:6: "And there shall be faith (*Zera'im*) in – your time (*Mo'ed*) a store (*Nashim*) of salvation (*Nezikin*) and wisdom (*Kodashim*) and knowledge (*Taharot*)."
39. Rav Sherira Gaon (op. cit.) and Rambam (*Introduction to Seder Zeraim*) have attempted to give some logical explanation for this apparent anomaly and also, for instance, why *Masechet Sukkot* precedes *Masechet Rosh Hashanah.* The explanation of Rambam is of a homiletic nature and that of Rav Sherira Gaon is incomplete in the available manuscripts. The first *Tosafot* in various *masechtot* are also concerned with this problem.
40. R. Margulies, *Yesod HaMishnah V'Arichatah* (Tel Aviv, 1956), which also provides an explanation for the difficulty presented by *Seder Zera'im* in this connection.
41. This is certainly true for five of the six *sedarim.* Note that originally the first three tractates of *Nezikin* formed a single *masechta* (**Bava Kama* 102a), as did also *Masech-*

A Conflict between a Mishnah That Is Anonymous and One That Is Not

It is of importance to know whether, in fact, the present sequence of *mishnayot* is identical with that which R. Yehudah haNasi followed in his studies, because, as has been stated, there are cases where the identical statement of *halachah* appears in two different *mishnayot*: in one *mishnah*, anonymously, and in another, as the statement of a particular *Tanna*.[42]

In such cases, it is important to establish which of the two *mishnayot* was studied first by R. Yehudah haNasi, the anonymous one or that which reports the individual's statement,[43] because the rule for ascertaining the *halachah* turns on the question: Which Mishnah did R. Yehudah haNasi study first?

If of the two *mishnayot* that which was first studied by R. Yehudah haNasi is anonymous,[44] it is assumed that this expressed his first decision of *halachah*, and that the second *mishnah* indicates that he had later revoked this decision. If the second of two *mishnayot* is anonymous, it is assumed that R. Yehudah haNasi had at first been uncertain and that the later *mishnah* reflects his final decision.[45]

---

tot Sanhedrin and *Makkot* (Rambam, op. cit.). Chapters 6 and 7 of *Masechet Tamid* must be counted as one chapter, which is in accordance with some manuscripts (H. Strack, *Introduction to Talmud and Midrash* [New York, 1959], p. 366, note 14).

42. For example, Mishnah *Sotah* 9:1 states: "In the case of *eglah arufah* (a red heifer), three judges used to come from the court in Jerusalem. R. Yehudah says five judges." Here then the requirement of three judges is stated anonymously. Mishnah *Sanhedrin* 1:3 states: "The case of *eglah arufah* is decided upon by three judges, says R. Shimon; R. Yehudah says five judges." Here then the requirement of three judges is reported as an individual view.

43. "The *mishnah* which was studied last is the decisive one." *Yevamot* 42b, **Bava Kama* 102a, *Avodah Zarah* 7a and *Niddah* 11b.

44. In the example given in footnote 42 above, *Sotah* (in *Seder Nashim*) takes precedence over *Sanhedrin* (in *Seder Nezikin*) in the sequence of *Mishnayot* so the *halachah* requiring three judges cannot be taken to have the support of R. Yehudah haNasi, if the present order of the *sedarim* is identical with that in which R. Yehudah haNasi studied. See Rashbam, *Bava Batra* 122b, "Rebbi changed his mind."

45. Rashi, *Avodah Zarah* 7a., as explained by *Divrei Sofrim* (Jerusalem, 1956), Part I, p. 77. According to R. Yehudah (*Bava Kama* 102a), it must be assumed that the present arrangement was that which R. Yehudah haNasi followed in his studies where it

Sufficient has been said to show that the Sages who were responsible for the arrangement of the Mishnah were responsible also for producing some elementary form of codification. Were these same Sages also responsible for reducing the Oral Law to writing? Were these arrangements of the Mishnah, which have been discussed, handed down by word of mouth or had they been committed to writing? These questions remain to be considered.

SECTION III: THE WRITING OF THE MISHNAH AND THE CHARACTER OF THE SAGES

Was the First Mishnaic Arrangement in Writing or Oral?

There are many references in the Talmud to scrolls[46] and correspondence[47] in writing, concerning matters of *halachah*,[48] notwithstanding the prohibition against writing down the Oral Law.[49] These written documents, however, were all for private use,[50] and the prohibition against writing down the Oral Law did not apply to these.[51] On the other hand, it is clear that the task of arranging the Mishnah had been undertaken in such a way as to achieve the maximum of publicity,

---

concerns two *mishnayot* in one *masechta*. When it comes however to two *masechtot* or two different *Sedarim*, there are many different opinions. For a general discussion of the problem, see **Tosefot Yom-Tov* on Mishnah *Sotah* 9:1. See also *Kesef Mishneh, Hilchot Rotze'ach* 9:1; *Tosafot, Shabbat* 81b and *Yevamot* 42b.

46. *Megillat Taanit* (Mishnah *Taanit* 2:8; *Eruvin* 62b), *Megillat Yochsin* (*Yevamot* 49b), *Megillat Samamonim* (*Yoma* 38a).
47. Letters from various Rabbis (*Shabbat* 116a, *Shevuot* 48b), a letter from Rovin (*Ketubot* 39a, *Bava Metzia* 114a), thirty-nine camels loaded with letters from Shemuel to R. Yochanan (*Chullin* 95b).
48. Concerning *Aggadah*, there is mention of a Book *of Aggadah* (*Berachot* 23a, *Bava Metzia* 116a).
49. *Gittin* 60b based on *Shemot* 34:27: "And the Eternal said to Moshe, 'Write for yourself these words, for according to these words have I made a covenant with you and with Israel.'" From this the Sages deduced "what is said orally must not be stated in writing."
50. They may be identical with the "hidden scrolls" to which the Talmud (*Shabbat* 6a) refers.
51. "No text books were composed for *public teaching* of the Oral Law. However, the

because its purpose was "that all teachers should cite the law in a uniform language and style."[52] The *mishnah* arrangement was therefore not for private use, and it is unlikely that this arrangement was in writing – unless by that time the prohibition against the writing down of the Oral Law had been suspended.

From comments made by both Rashi[53] and the Tosafists,[54] it would appear that even by R. Yehudah's time, the prohibition against writing down the Oral Law for public study had not yet been lifted. Rambam,[55] however, refers to "Rebbi," who collected the traditional teachings and wrote them all down."

The Early Sages and the Later Sages

Whether the Oral Law had been written down by the end of the Mishnaic period or not, in any event with the conclusion of the Mishnah a great epoch in the development of the law came to a close. Just as the Sages of the Mishnah had accepted that they have no power to abrogate Sinaitic Law,[56] so the teachers of the Talmud considered themselves bound by the ruling of the Mishnah.[57] It appears that the later Sages felt that they

prophet or head of *Bet Din* of each generation would create notes for his own use of what he had heard from his teachers and would himself teach orally in public" (Rambam, *Mishneh Torah*, Introduction).

52. *Iggeret Rav Sherira Gaon.*
53. See *Shabbat* 13b and *Eruvin* 62b: "Nothing except *Megillat Ta'anit* had been reduced to writing" in the days of Abaye. See also *Bava Metzia* 33a: "Later generations started writing it down."
54. *Megillah* 32a. Talmudists would chant the Mishnah, because it was not reduced to writing and the tune helped the memory.
55. Op. cit.
56. See p. 102.
57. See *Kesef Mishneh* on Rambam's *Hilchot Mamrim* 2:1: "Why do the *Amoraim* not dispute with the *Tanna'im*...? It seems that after the conclusion of the Mishnah the later generations undertook not to dispute with the earlier generations. A similar thing occurred at the conclusion of the Talmud." After the conclusion of the Talmud, it was not even possible to enact new *Takkanot* and *Gezerot* for the whole of Jewry. See Rambam, Introduction to *Mishneh Torah.*

did not possess the greatness of the earlier Sages and that therefore their power to act as law-makers was more limited.[58]

Throughout this book we have spoken of the contribution of the Sages to the Oral Law without reference to the character of the Sages who were the law makers. It would be well if in conclusion we made the remark that the greatness of the Sages to which we have just referred did not lie in any particular office or appointment which they occupied or held, nor did it rest entirely on intellectual superiority or erudition.[59] More than that was required of the Sages. "If the teacher is like an angel of God," said the Sages, "seek Torah from him; and if not, do not seek Torah from him."[60]

A New Theory Why the Law Was Not to Be Put into Writing

The emphasis laid upon the spiritual quality of the teachers of the Oral Law and not merely on the quality of their teaching is one of the more distinctive features of traditional Judaism.[61] It may also be one of the

58. The thought that earlier generations were greater is variously expressed in Talmudic literature – see *Shabbat* 112b: "If the earlier generations were like angels, we are like mere men"; *Eruvin* 53a: "The heart of earlier generations was like the gate of the *Ulam* (20 *amot*) and that of the later generations like the gate of the Temple (10 *amot*)"; *Yoma* 9b. See generally, Simcha Lieberman's *Taamei HaMitzvot* of Rabbi Menachem of Recanati (London, 1962), p. 20 et seq.
59. See *Sukkah* 28a (Soncino Talmud): "Hillel the elder had eighty disciples...the greatest of them was Yonatan ben Uziel and the least of them Yochanan ben Zakkai. They said of R. Yochanan ben Zakkai that he did not leave unstudied Scripture, Mishnah, Gemara, Halachah, *Aggadah,* details of the scribes... They said of Yonatan ben Uziel that when he used to sit and occupy himself with the Torah, every bird that flew above him was immediately burned." (It was like at Mount Sinai when the Torah was given in fire. – *Tosafot.*)

    Notwithstanding R. Yochanan's scholarship, the "greatest" was the pupil who possessed the "fire of Sinai."
60. *Chagigah* 15b.
61. This is also one of the important "parting of the ways" of the traditional attitude to the Oral Law from the attitude of such writers as I.H. Weiss, who heaps abuse upon great *Tanna'im* throughout his work *Dor Dor V'Dorshav* (e.g. Vol. II, chs. 8 and 9, where he heaps abuse on R. Gamliel, R. Elazar and R. Yehoshua).

reasons why it was prohibited to write down the Oral Law.[62] The writing down of the law enables any scholar, whatever his character or his bias, to present himself as an interpreter and teacher of the Oral Law.[63] On the other hand, when the law is handed down orally, it is unlikely that teaching would be accepted from anyone whose character is not such as to make his tradition reliable. When there is no text against which it is possible to check the law which is being taught, the complete integrity of the teacher is the only assurance that what is being taught is not pure invention and fabrication. Therefore, it may be that the prohibition against committing the Oral Law to writing was intended to preserve the high spiritual qualities of the teachers of Oral Law. This idea is possibly contained in the Midrash[64] which states: "God said to Moshe Rabbenu, 'I will make you write most of my Torah but not all'...because the Mishnah is the mystery of God, and God hands over His mysteries only to the righteous."

---

62. See also *Sefer HaIkkarim* 3:23 and *Yam Shel Shlomo*, Introduction to *Chullin*, for suggestions as to why it was prohibited to commit the Oral Law to writing.
63. Making Torah too widely and easily accessible is fraught with danger. Furthermore, *Megillah* 3a states: "Eretz Yisrael shook for four hundred *parsa* by four hundred *parsa* and a *Bat Kol* came forth and demanded, 'Who has revealed My secrets to men,'" when Yonatan ben Uziel first translated *Nevi'im*.
64. *Midrash Tanchuma, Parashat Vayera* 6 (Buber edition).

Notes of Rav Simcha Wasserman זצ"ל

א. הייתי רוצה להסב את תשומת לבך לרש"י עירובין כ"א ע"ב, שם מוזכר ששלמה המלך עשה "מסורה" [בדיקה מדוקדקת של מילים ואותיות] למשנה, וזה מורה שהיה קיים נוסח של משנה לפני תקופת שלמה המלך. למעשה רש"י [משפטים כ"א,א] מציין שכבר בתחילת מסירת התורה, מסר אותה משה רבינו ע"י לימוד נוסחא של משנה...משנתו הכילה תמצית של כל ההלכות [זה מה שרי"א הלוי מכנה: יסוד המשנה]. ההוספות לנוסחא נעשו מאוחר יותר ע"י התנאים כדי לבאר וכו' [מתוך מכתב למחה"ס]

[הערת העורך: רי"א הלוי עצמו מזכיר כמה פעמים שיסוד המשנה נסדר מהימים היותר ראשונים ומסתימת לשונו אין נראה שלדעתו כך נמסר למשה מסיני. ובדוחק יש להבין כוונתו בעיקר לגבי תקנות חכמים הקדומות כמו איסורי השבותין ומוקצה דשבת ושניות לעריות ודומיהן שכל אחד ניתקן בשעתו ונשקע אז ביסוד המשנה, משא"כ ביאורי דיני התורה אולי שפיר נמסרו למשה בלשון משנה.]

ב. וכולהו אליבא דר"ע זהו בנוסחת המשנה עם ההוספות. [נראה כוונתו ע"ד שכתב בהערה דלעיל דיסוד נוסח המשנה קדום ורק ההוספות מאת התנאים לזה קאמר דהוספות אלה אליבא דר' עקיבא.]

ג. צריך לעיין באבות דר' נתן. [אולי כוונת הרש"ו עפ"י מה שכתב רש"י בגיטין דף ס"ז. ד"ה אוצר בלום לבאר כוונת האדר"ן, דר"ע עשה כל התורה מטבעות מטבעות, סידר מדרש ספרי וספרא לבדן והלכות לעצמן ואגדות לעצמן. וזאת בניגוד לר' טרפון שהושוה לגל של אגוזים כיון שהיה שונה הכל ביחד. ולא הוזכר כלום בענין עריכת נוסח המשנה.]

ד. כל ענין במשנה שמורה. [הכוונה דכל הענינים שנמסרו כתורה שבע"פ למשה רבינו, נשמרו במסורה של נוסח תמציתי הנקרא משנה וגם היא כבר נמסרה ע"י משה רבינו לכלל ישראל כמבואר בהערה א.]

ה. שני הסגנונים היו מאז, תושבע"פ ופי' תושב"כ.

ומה היה ענין המשנה בדורות הראשונים?

צריך לדעת כי יש ב׳ מיני מסורת בע״פ: מסורת ענינים ומסורת נוסחאות. מסורת ענינים היינו שחובת התלמיד לזכור ענין כל מה שלמד מרבו, מבלי שתהא עליו חובה לזכור גם נוסחת רבו והמילים שבו מסר לו הענינים, וכן בלמדו הוא לתלמידיו הרשות בידו להסביר להם בכל נוסחא שימצא לנכון לפניו, אך ורק בתנאי שישמור לדייק על עצם הענין, שידע אותו ושימסרנו לבאים אחריו בדיוק נכון.

מסורת נוסחאות היינו שחובת התלמיד לדעת גם את הנוסחא של רבו בדיוק ולמוסרה לתלמידיו באותם המילים ממש כמו שקיבל מרבו. והנה ב׳ האופנים יש בהן מגרעות: מסורת הענינים סכנה כרוכה בה שמתוך שכ״א מבין הענין לפי כשרונו ולפי טבעו, שהרי ב׳ תלמידים המבינים שניהם את רבם, מ״מ ברור שאין תפיסת האחד דומה ממש ולגמרי לתפיסת חבירו, וא״כ אילו נמסרה מסורת תושבע״פ באופן זה לחוד, החששא היתה גדולה שבמשך הדורות יפלו שינויים במסורה באופן שהיתה מקבלת פנים חדשות ח״ו, גם אופן מסורת הנוסחא אינו מספיק למסורת תושבע״פ, כי אופן מסורת זו מכביד על הזכרון ואינו אפשרי אלא לכמות מועטה, וברור שא״א הוא למסורת התורה אשר ארוכה מארץ מדה ורחבה מני ים.

אשר ע״כ באמת מסורת תושבע״פ כפולה, עצם המסורת עצמה נמסרה רק באופן של מסורת ענינים, והיא מסורת הגמרא. במסורת זו כל הענינים נמסרים מרב לתלמיד בכל רחבם והיקפם, גדריהם וטעמיהם, באופן די להבין הענינים על בורים כדי להבין דבר מתוך דבר. ולא זו בלבד אלא שבאופן מסורת זו נמסר מהתחלתו בנוסח של ויכוחים והיקשים, אתקפתות ופירוקיהן, היינו שהרב אעפ״י שידע ההלכה בבירור, לא אמרה פשוט לתלמידיו, אלא שהעלה אותה מתוך פלפולה של תורה. והתוצאות הן שתים, הבנת הענינים התלבנה והתבררה מתוך כך, ועוד לימוד זה התכוין גם לפתח השכל שיהא מוכשר לדמות ולחלק, כמבואר ברמב״ם ושו״ע על שליש בתלמוד.

ולא די בזה אלא שעוד, כל עניני תושבע״פ נתכנסו לתוך נוסחאות קצרות שבקצרות, מועט מחזיק את המרובה, ושוב כל עניני תושבע״פ נמסרו מפה לאוזן גם במסורת הנוסחא, משניות, שבהן היו כלולות כל ההלכות, ושאותן צריך היה לדעת באותיותיהן ממש, כמו ששמע וקיבל כ״א מרבו, ועל זה אמרו חכמים שחייב אדם לומר בלשון רבו, היינו בלא שינוי משהו, ומסורת זו שימשה שמירה וגדר למסורת הגמ׳ שתשמור את פניה האמיתיים כקבלתה מסיני.

ו. דבר זה נאמר שם בענין גזירת גבינה של גוים ואין ראיה משם לדרך הסגנון.

Hebrew Sources

SECTION I

The First Mishnah Arrangement

4. Iggeret Rav Sherira Gaon, p. 39

וספרא וספרי דרשי דקראי אינון והיכא רמיזא הלכתא בקראי, ומעיקרא במקדש שני ביומי דרבנן קמאי לפום הדין אורחא הווי תני להון.

7. Tosefta, Eduyot 1:1

כשנכנסו חכמים לכרם ביבנה אמרו עתידה שעה שיהא אדם מבקש דבר מדברי תורה ואינו מוצא, מדברי סופרים ואינו מוצא, שנאמר (עמוס ח׳) הנה ימים באים נאם ה׳ וגו׳ ישוטטו לבקש את דבר ה׳ ולא ימצאו... שלא יהא דבר מדברי תורה דומה לחבירו. אמרו נתחיל מהלל ושמאי...

10. Sanhedrin 86a

סתם מתני׳ ר׳ מאיר, סתם תוספתא ר׳ נחמיה, סתם ספרא ר׳ יהודה, סתם ספרי ר״ש וכלהו אליבא דר״ע.

15. Sha'arei Teshuvah 1:20

מימות משה רבינו עד הלל הזקן היו שש מאות סדרי משנה כמו שנתנם הקב״ה למשה בסיני, ומן הלל ואילך נתמעט ונתמסכן העולם וחלש כבודה של תורה ולא תקנו מהלל ושמאי אלא ששה סדרים בלבד.

19. R' I.I. Halevy, Dorot HaRishonim 1:3, p. 206

והנה בית שמאי ובית הלל הם הנם הדור הראשון לתקופת התנאים, והם הנם הראשונים אשר באו מהם במשנה מחלקאות ואשר מזה טעו לחשוב שהם היו מיסדי ההלכה.

כי על כן עלינו רק לפתוח את ספר המשנה, לראות על מה ילכו שם כל דבריהם.

לדוגמא במס׳ אהלות ז׳ משנה ג׳ ״המת בבית ולו פתחים הרבה כולן טמאים נפתח אחד מהם הוא טמא וכולן טהורים, חשב להוציאו באחד מהם או בחלון שהוא ארבעה על ארבעה טפחים הציל על כל הפתחים.

בית שמאי אומרים והוא שחשב עד שלא ימות המת ובית הלל אומרים אף משמת״.

ומי לא יראה כי דברי בית שמאי ובית הלל אינם כי אם מה שנחלקו בפרוש כונת דברי המשנה במה שנאמר בה ״חשב להוציאו״ שבית שמאי סוברין שהכונה שחשב עוד טרם שימות המת, ובית הלל מפרשים דין המשנה שהוא גם בכל האופנים, וגם את חשב משמת.

ומחלוקות כאלה יבואו לפנינו גם בדברי מפרשי המשנה, רק שדברי התנאים בכל כיוצא בזה נקבעו אחר זה על המשנה ובאו לפנינו סדורים עמה יחד.

22. Iggeret Rav Sherira Gaon, p.28

ולא הוו חד מן הראשונים דכתב מדעם עד סוף יומי דרבינו הקדוש. וכן נמי לא הוו גרסי כולא בפה אחד ולשון אחד אלא טעמייהו הוו ידעין להון וכלהון דעת אחת הוה בהון ואל הות בגריסיהו פלוגתא וידעי מאי דאיתיה דברי הכל ומאי דאית ביה פלוגתא ומאי דאיתיה ליחיד ומאי דאיתיה לרבים ולא היו להם דברים מתוקנים ומשנה ידוע שהכל שונין אותה בפה אחד ולשון אחד. אלא אותן הטעמים והשמועות שהיו יודעין אע״פ שהחכמים כולן היו שוין בהם, כל אחד ואחד מתני לתלמידיו באי זה חבור שירצה ובאיזה דרך שירצה יש שאוחז דרך קצרה... ושקטו רבנן ביומי דרבי מכל שמדא משום רחמנותא דאיכא בין אנטונינוס ורבי ואסכים לתרוצי הלכתא כי היכי דלגרסי רבנן כולהו פה אחד ולשון אחד ולא לגרוס כל חד וחד לישנא לנפשיה.

SECTION II

Clarification of the Oral Law at Yavneh

31. Bava Metzia 59b

מאי עכנאי אמר ר״י אמר שמואל שהקיפו דברים כעכנא זו וטמאוהו. תנא באותו היום השיב רבי אליעזר כל תשובות שבעולם ולא קבלו הימנו אמר להם אם הלכה כמותי חרוב זה יוכיח נעקר חרוב ממקומו מאה אמה ואמרי לה ארבע מאות אמה. אמרו לו אין מביאין ראיה מן החרוב. חזר ואמר להם אם הלכה כמותי אמת המים

יוכיחו. חזרו אמת המים לאחוריהם. אמרו לו אין מביאין ראיה מאמת המים. חזר ואמר להם אם הלכה כמותי כותלי בית המדרש יוכיחו הטו כותלי בית המדרש ליפול, גער בהם ר' יהושע... יצאתה בת קול ואמרה מה לכם אצל ר"א שהלכה כמותו בכ"מ עמד ר"י על רגליו ואמר לא בשמים היא. מאי לא בשמים היא? אמר רבי ירמיה שכבר נתנה תורה מהר סיני. אין אנו משגיחין בבת קול שכבר כתבת בהר סיני בתורה "אחרי רבים להטות"... אותו היום הביאו כל טהרות שטיהר ר"א ושרפום באש ונמנו עליו וברכוהו.

32. Berachot 27b

ת"ר מעשה בתלמיד אחד שבא לפני ר' יהושע, א"ל "תפילת ערבית רשות או חובה"? א"ל "רשות". בא לפני רבן גמליאל א"ל תפילת ערבית רשות או חובה"? א"ל "חובה". א"ל "והלא ר"י אמר לי רשות" א"ל "המתן עד שיכנסו בעלי תריסין לבית המדרש" כשנכנסו בעלי תריסין עמד השואל ושאל "תפילת ערבית רשות או חובה"? א"ל ר"ג "חובה". אמר להם ר"ג לחכמים "כלום יש אדם שחולק בדבר זה". אמר ליה ר"י "לאו!" א"ל "והלא משמך אמרו לי רשות!" אמר ליה "יהושע עמוד על רגליך ויעידו בך"... היה ר"ג יושב ודורש ור"י עומד על רגליו עד שרננו כל העם ואמרו לחוצפית התורגמן "עמוד!" ועמד. אמרו "עד כמה נצעריה וניזיל, בר"ה אשתקד צעריה, בבכורות במעשה דר, צדוק צעריה, הכא נמי צעריה, תא ונעבריה!"

The Redaction of R. Yehudah haNasi

34. Gittin 29a

מתני' המביא גט בא"י וחלה, ה"ז משלחו ביד אחר. ואם א"ל טול לי הימנה חפץ פלוני, לא ישלחנו ביד אחר, שאין רצונו שיהא פקדונו ביד אחר. גמ' אמר ר"ל כאן שנה רבי אין השואל רשאי להשאיל, ואין השוכר רשאי להשכיר.

43. Bava Kama 102a

מתני': הנותן צמר... לצבוע לו אדם וצבעו שחור, שחור וצבעו אדום, ר"מ אומר נותן לו דמי צמרו, ר"י אומר אם השבח יתר על היציאה נותן לו את היציאה יתירה על השבח נותן לו את השבח.

גמ': ויתיב רב הונא וקאמר... והלכה כר"י... אהדרינהו רב יוסף לאפיה... למה לי... מחלוקת ואחר כך סתם הלכה כסתם! מחלוקת בבבא קמא... וסתם בבבא מציעא, דתנן כל המשנה ידו על התחתונה... ורב הונא אצטרך, סד"א אין סדר למשנה וסתם ואחר כך מחלוקת היא. ורב יוסף? אי הכי כל מחלוקת ואח"כ סתמא

נימא אין סדר למשנה וסתם ואח״כ מחלוקת היא. ורב הונא כי לא אמרינן אין סדר למשנה בחדא מסכתא אבל בתרי מסכתות אמרינן.

45. Tosefot Yom-Tov, Sotah 9:1

ותירצו (בתוספות) דאע״ג דלכולהו אמוראי בתרי מסכתות אין סדר ואין הלכה כסתם ר׳ יוחנן אית ליה דאפילו בתרי מסכתות הלכה כסתם. דמסתמא סתם לבסוף ואין לנו לומר שסתם רבי קודם ושוב חזר ממה שפסק ע״כ... נ״ל... שהרמב״ם מתרץ קושית התוס׳ בכך דלהכי מקשה גמרא מסתם דבנזיר אע״ג דמחלוקת היא בביצה משום דכיון דבתרי סדרי נינהו. ונזיר בסדר נשים שאחר סדר מועד אמרינן דיש סדר והוה מחלוקת ואחר כך סתם דהלכה כסתם. וטעמא רבה איכא דכיון דנקטינן בסידרייהו באסמכתא דקרא (ישעיה ל״ג) ״והיה אמונת עתך״ כדאיתא בפ״ב דשבת (דף לב) אית לן למימר דכסדר האסמכתא למדם רבינו הקודש... ומיהו לדעת הרי״ף והרא״ש נמי אין סדר אפילו בתרי סדרי.

Afterword

The Talmud and the *Talmid*

We have discussed extensively how morality and *ve'ahavta lere'acha kamocha* are relevant to the development of the Oral Torah. But it is equally relevant to the development of the student of Oral Law. Hillel teaches us that the idea of *ve'ahavta lere'acha kamocha* encompasses the whole Torah; it is "*kol hatorah kulah*" – the entire Torah, and the rest is merely detail.[1] Chazal taught us: "*Lo nitnah mitzvot ela letzaref bahen et habriot*" – the purpose of mitzvot is to refine the character of the student.[2] The teacher has to teach the *Talmid* (pupil) to work on his character. "What he is" is as important as "what he does."

This is borne out by the Sages, who, as we have seen, say: "Just as He is kind, so must you be kind."[3] It is not good enough to do charity and to perform a kindness. The student must learn to be generous and to have empathy for the "other."

How to teach a student of Torah to prioritize *ve'ahavta lere'acha kamocha* is not a new problem. There was a dispute in the yeshiva world when Rabbi Yisrael Salanter established the *mussar* movement. He thought the students were concentrating on *mitzvot bein adam l'makom*

---

1. *Shabbat* 31a.
2. *Midrash Tanchuma, Shmini,* chapter 12.
3. *Masechet Sofrim* 3:17.

but were lax in *mitzvot bein adam l'chaveiro*. He sought to arrest this tendency by introducing a dedicated study of *mussar* (morality). The *Bet Midrash* of Volozhin had a strong objection to this change. Their view was that the study of Torah in itself is sufficient to teach morality. When Rabbi Sabato asked Rabbi Aharon Lichtenstein *zt"l* for his attitude to these conflicting views, Rabbi Lichtenstein commented: "The idea that it is possible to achieve full spiritual and moral sustenance through the discussions of Abaye and Rava, and that one has no need for anything external, may have been true in Volozhin, but even there it was only true for some of the students and not all of them."[4]

I am in no way competent to "put my head in between two mountains," the *Bet Midrash* of Volozhin and the *Bet Midrash* of Rabbi Yisrael Salanter. It seems to me, however, that there is an argument to be made that *mussar* should not be treated as a holy subject and confined to the *Bet Midrash* and to certain hours of study. Morality must be shown to be a part of the discussion of Abaye and Rava. In the study of the Talmud, morality – or, shall we say, *ve'ahavta lere'acha kamocha* – must be a part of that study.

A *rebbe* and a *talmid* will often come across statements of the Sages that seems problematic and opposed to basic moral principles, such as those we discussed earlier under the heading "Moral *Svara* and *Halachot* Which Seem Immoral." It is important that if the *talmid* asks the question: "Rebbe, is this fair?" it is not treated as the question of an ignorant layman. "Rebbe, is this fair?" is a "*lomdish*" question. As we have shown, *halachah* produced by the Sages is both fair and equitable, and the student must be made aware of that. Moreover, in these situations the *rebbe* should not wait for the *talmid* to ask the question; it is for the teacher to initiate the discussion on the question raised by these statements of the Sages – and any similar statements.[5]

I do not imagine that anything that we have said in this afterword

---

4. Haim Sabato, *Seeking His Presence: Conversations with Rabbi Aharon Lichtenstein* (Tel Aviv, 2016), 86.
5. A teacher must take great care to avoid the risk of putting off his *talmid* from Talmudic studies for the rest of his life.
   If the *talmid* is told that a *halachah* follows logically from a *drash* – when in fact it

can hope to reach anywhere near the eloquence of the Sages, who say it all in far fewer words:

> "*Ve'ahavta et Hashem Elokecha*" – this means that the name of God should become loved through you. One should read and study and serve Torah scholars. One should deal with people calmly. What do people say about such a person? Praised be his father who taught him Torah. Praised be his teacher who taught him Torah. Woe to the people who do not learn Torah. This person who was taught Torah, see how pleasant are his ways, how proper are his deeds. Regarding such a person it is written: "And He said to me, you are My servant, Israel, in whom I will be glorified" (Is. 49:3).[6]

---

does not (see Chapter 2, Section II), or that a *svara* is logic – when it is not (see Section III), or that a *Ha'aramah* allows one to do what would otherwise have been prohibited by the Torah – when it does not (see Chapter 6), there is a real risk.

6. *Yoma* 86a.

Index of Sources and Authorities

Abarbanel, *Yehoshua* 7:19–20 96
Ancient Law (Maine), p. 25 113
Aruch HaShulchan 304:11 127
Atvun d'Oraita 54
Avot D'Rabbi Natan 18: 138
Ayelet HaShachar (Malbim) 33, 45
Bartenura
    Mishnah *Eduyot* 1:5 103
    Mishnah *Avot* 1:1 85, 90
    Mishnah *Yadayim* 4:3 14
Beit Yosef, Orach Chayim 530 28
Bible
    Shemot
        9:15 120
        12:15 4
        13:17 119
        16:19 37
        20:10 38
        20:13 38, 85
        21:1 4
        23:13 37
        31:14 3, 19
        34:27 34, 149
    Vayikra
        1:4 12
        6:13 33
        18:18 136
        19:2 125
        19:10 141

19:14 50
22:14 141
22:28 115
23:39–40 30
24:11–14 96
25:35 123
27:31 119
29:4 2
Bemidbar 27:1 5
Devarim
4:2 99
5:27 121
7:3–4 121
12:13 96
12:21 3, 22
15:1–2 117
15:31 84
16:8 4
17:8–10 34, 69
17:10 87
17:11 87
18:16 95
19:16–19 53
21:18–21 52
22:8 51
24:1–4 4, 19
24:14 51
24:16 29
24:21 141
Yehoshua
7:19–20 96
8:30–31 96
Shoftim
6:25–27 96
13:19 96
Shemuel I 15:22 98
Shemuel II 1:5, 9–10 96, 97
Melachim I 18:20–24 95, 96
Yeshayahu
1:11–15 98

1:13 98
33:6 147
Yirmeyahu 7:9 98
Hoshea 6:6 98
Amos 5:22–24 98
Michah 6:7 98
Tehillim 119:126 95
Mishlei
2:20 125
3:17 51
Chatam Sofer Resp. *Orach Chayim* 208 15
Chavot Yair Resp. 192 14
Chayei Adam, klal 10:1 73
Chazon Ish, Collected Letters
Part I, 33 15
Part II, p. 24 10
Cheker V'iyun Vol. I, p. 32 27
Concise Law Dictionary (Osborn) 113
Darkei HaMishnah
p. 15 138
p. 221 138
Die Erste Mischna 1, 5, 7, 81, 136, 138
Dikdukei Sofrim 84
Divrei Chayim Yoreh Deah II, resp. 105 2
Divrei David, Vayikra 24:12 96
Divrei Sofrim
p. 8 32
p. 77 148
Dor Dor V'Dorshav Vol. II, chs. 8–9 151
Dorot HaRishonim
1:3
p. 206 139, 155
p. 220 62, 76
p. 223 61, 76
p. 311 61, 62
1:5
p. 467 30
p. 487 33, 46
p. 514–542 37

p. 516 16
p. 525 34
p. 543 141
Encounter
p. 76 127
p. 102 127
Gur Aryeh, Yitro 32, 33, 34, 44
Haamek Sheeilah 47(I) 28
Halakhic Morality 54
HaTalmud uMadai'i HaTevel p. 111 2
Hirsch, S. R., *Shemot* 21:2 4
Historical Introduction to English Law, p. 207 114
Iggeret Rav Sherira Gaon 150
p. 28 141, 156
p. 32 143, 147
p. 39 136, 155
Igrot Moshe
Orach Chayim, resp. 14 94
Yoreh De'ah 2:128 75
Choshen Mishpat 1:60 127
Intercom (Rosenfeld), Vol. Ill, no. 3 120
Introduction to Roman Law, p. 23 114
Introduction to Talmud and Midrash, p. 366 148
Israel Law Review Vol. 9, no. 4, p. 542 38
Iyyunim BeMishnato shel HaRambam, chs. 3–4 36
Journal of a Rabbi, p. 229 2
Kach Darko shel Talmud, p. 26 116
Kesef Mishneh
Hilchot Mamrim 2:1 150
Hilchot Rotze'ach 9:1 149
Hilchot Yesodei HaTorah 9:4 94
Kimchi, *Tehillim* 119:126 95
Kinat Sofrim, Sefer HaMitzvot, Shoresh 2 37
Kiryat Sefer, Introduction 27, 36
Kitvei Maharal miPrague Vol. II, p. 284 30
Kovetz Biurim, Shev Shmatese 9 87, 91
Kovetz Ma'amarim v'Igrot part III, p. 298 15
Kovetz Shiurim part II, ch. 3 39

Kuntres Divrei Sofrim
- 1:17–24 — 39
- p. 6 — 72, 79
- p. 8 — 32

Kuzari, Ma'amar 3
- par. 35 — 4, 19
- par. 73 — 29, 32

Lechem Mishneh, Hilchot Mamrim
- 2:3 — 105
- 7:11 — 52

Leo Jung Jubilee Volume, p. 155 — 146
Lev Same'ach, Sefer HaMitzvot, Shoresh 2 — 37
Maggid Mishneh, Hilchot Shechenim 14:5 — 126, 132
Maharam ibn Chaviv, *Sefer Get Pashut, Klal* 1 — 16
Maharatz Chajes
- *Darkei HaHora'ah* II — 102, 123
- *Mavo HaTalmud*
  - Ch. 1 — 31
  - p. 58 — 61, 62, 68
  - p. 298 — 76
- *Torat HaNevi'im, Eleh HaMitzvot*, Ch. 1 — 95, 96

Maoz HaDat, p. 12 — 32
Margoliot HaYam — 84
Mavo LaMishnah
- p. 65 — 140
- p. 82 — 137, 140

Mavo l'Torah sheBichtav vsheBe'al Peh — 63
Megillat Esther, Sefer HaMitzvot
- *Shoresh* 1 — 10, 14
- *Shoresh* 2 — 37, 40

Meiri
- *Bava Metzia* 83a — 127
- *Yevamot* 90b — 95
- *Sanhedrin*
  - 52b — 97
  - 89b — 97
- *Avodah Zarah* 36a — 103, 105

Mekor Chayim 448:11 — 120
Melechet Machshevet, p. 134 et seq. — 66, 77

Meshech Chochmah, Devarim
30:12 85
17:11 71, 78
Metzudat David, Yeshayahu 1:13 98
Midrashim
Shemot Rabbah 41 7
Vayikra Rabbah
29:4 2
32:1 9
Bemidbar Rabbah 14:1 96
Kohelet Rabbah 1:9 7
Tanchuma 152
Yalkut Tehillim 9 147
Minchat Chinuch, Mitzvah 516 97
Mishnah
Pe'ah
7:4 141
7:7 141
Shevi'it 7:3 67
Terumot
6:1 140
6:6 141
8:4, 5 67
Ma'aser Sheni 4:4 119, 130
Orlah 1:2 5, 20
Shabbat
2:1 63
3:1 62, 63
4:1 62
6:1 62
Pesachim
2:2 119
6:1 102
8:8 102
Beitzah 5:2 62
Taanit 2:8 149
Chagigah 2:2 12, 23
Yevamot
1:1 135

8:3 13, 23, 30
12:6 136
Ketubot
2:3 29
4:1 35
Nedarim 5:6 119, 130
Sotah
8:1–2 136
9:1 148
Gittin
5:6 146
5:8 68, 70
Kiddushin 1:1 36, 122, 139
Bava Kama
10:2 68
10:9 65
Bava Batra 8:3 5, 20
Sanhedrin
1:3 148
1:4 136
2:4 136
4:5 136
6:2 136
Makkot 2:4 5, 20
Eduyot 1:5 16, 103, 110
Avodah Zarah 1:7 67
Chullin 2:5 67
Kritot 3:9 13
Kelim 30:4 144
Ohalot
7:3 139
18:9 146
Negaim
7:1 5, 19
9:3 13
11:7 13
12:5 136
Yadayim 4:3 14
Mitzvot Hashem p. 108, *klal* 17 74

Mordechai, Bava Metzia 24b 127
Nemukei Yosef
    Yevamot 88a 102
    Sanhedrin 52b 97
Netivat HaMishpat 234 87
Noda B'yehuda Vol II, *Yoreh De'ah* 36 52
Ohr HaChayim Vayikra 13:34 30, 32, 43
Ohr Same'ach, Hilchot Mamrim 2:9 100
Ohr Zarua, Sukkah 306 16
Pri Chadash
    Petichah Kolelet
        Orach Chayim 1:2 74
        Yoreh De'ah 116 111
Ra'avad
    Hilchot Mamrim
        2:2 103
        2:9 97, 100
    Sefer HaKabbalah 9, 21, 63
Rabbeinu Chananel, *Sukkah* 45b 8, 21
Radbaz, *Hilchot Mamrim* 2:2 103
Ralbag, *Yeshoshua* 7:19–20 96
Rambam
    Commentary to Mishnah
        Avot 1:3 15
        Sukkah 4:9 14
        Sanhedrin 24:4 97
        Kelim 17:12 37
        Mikvaot 7:7 37
    Hilchot Avadim 9:7 57
    Hilchot Mamrim
        1:2 70
        1:4 17
        2:1 36
        2:2 103
        2:3 105
        2:4 97
        2:5 104
        2:9 100, 108
    Hilchot Me'ilah 8:8 58

Hilchot Shabbat 12:8 39
Hilchot Teshuvah 3:8 84, 90
Hilchot Yesodei HaTorah
9:3 95, 96
9:4 94, 107
Hilchot Yom Tov 2:4 116
Introduction to Mishneh Torah 150
Introduction to Seder Zera'im 7, 11, 13, 16, 21, 24, 30, 32, 42, 147, 148
Moreh Nevuchim 32
3:34 124, 131
Sanhedrin, Perek Chelek (Introduction) 82, 89
Sefer HaMitzvot
Shoresh 1 70, 77, 85, 90
Shoresh 2 30, 34, 46
Thirteen Principles of Faith 94
Ramban
Vayikra
19:2 125, 132
28:29 29
Devarim
4:2 100, 108
17:11 2, 18
Shabbat 3a 39
Bava Batra 12a 2, 15, 18
Sefer HaMitzvot
Shoresh 1 16, 70, 78
Shoresh 2 36, 37, 46
Ran
Yoma 1:1 28, 41
Nedarim 8a 34
Sanhedrin
46a 97
59b 103
Avodah Zarah 36a 105
Sermons of the Ran
Sermon 7 38
Sermon 11 57
Rashba
Rosh Hashanah 16b 101, 109
Shabbat 31a 55

Responsa 5:238 97
Rashbam, Bava Batra 122b 148
Rashi
Shemot 21:1 153
Vayikra 19:14 51
Berachot
5a 16
20b 32
47b 16
Shabbat
117b 115
132a 75
Eruvin
21b 153
96a 101
Pesachim 42b 52
Yoma 69a 95
Beitzah 5a 121
Moed Katan 17a 51
Yevamot 90b 95
Sotah
22a 16
47b 16
Gittin
36a 117, 129
67a 153
Kiddushin 57b 30
Bava Metzia 83a 127
Avodah Zarah 7a 148
Menachot 67a 123
Chullin 16a 29
Remah, *Sanhedrin* 78b 96
Ritva, *Rosh Hashanah* 16a 32, 44
Rosh
Introduction to Mikvaot 14
Responsa 2:8 103
Samuel Mirsky Jubilee Volume (Weinberg) 140
Sdei Chemed 3, p. 282 127
Sefer HaChinuch, Mitzvah 454 100

Sefer HaIkkarim
- 3:14 — 100
- 3:23 — 7, 152

Sefer Kritut — 144
Seridei Eish part IV, p. 225 — 15
Sha'arei Teshuvah 1:20 — 138, 155
Shakh, *Yoreh De'ah* 242 — 16
Shiltei HaGiborim, Mishnah *Rosh Hashanah* 4 — 101
Shitah Mekubetzet, Bava Metzia
- 24b — 127
- 83a — 127

Shnei Luchot HaBrit
- *Masechet Shevuot* — 32
- *Bet Chochmah* 28:2 — 73
- *Torah sheBe'al Peh* — 28, 32, 41
- *Torah sheBichtav*, p. 58b — 126

Shulchan Aruch
- *Orach Chayim* 448:3 — 120
- *Yoreh De'ah* 240 — 127
- *Even HaEzer* 112 — 67

Shulchan Aruch haRav, Hilchot Talmud Torah 2:12–13 — 82
Shvitat Asur 2:10 — 73
Sifra
- *Vayikra*
  - 3:14 — 51
  - 6:13 — 33
- *Behar* — 7, 20

Sifrei, Devarim
- sec. 55 — 100
- sec. 68 — 95
- sec. 229 — 51

Soncino Talmud, Sukkah 28a — 151
Taamei HaMitzvot, p. 20 — 151
Talmud (Babylonian)
- *Berachot*
  - 5a — 7, 20
  - 20b — 36
  - 21a — 35
  - 21b — 31, 43

23a 149
27b 145, 157
31a 119, 130
33b 120
35a 50, 58
48b 60
54a 95
63a 95

Shabbat
6a 149
13b 150
14b 60, 61
15a 64, 67
23a 70, 77
30a 60
31a 3, 55, 147
40a 65
46a 146
59b 62
73a 38
82b 31
88a 34
88b 72
96b 28, 42
103b 14
104a 11
110a 62
112b 151
116a 149
117b 115, 129
130b 102
132a 75
135a 30
150a 62

Eruvin
4b 14, 30
13b 144
17a 60
31b 29
53a 151

62b 149, 150
77a 35
79a 142
Pesachim
4b 35
18b 36
46b 115
66a 11, 84
81b 30
120a 4
Yoma
9b 151
14b 142
16a 142
38a 149
69a 95
81a 11
82a 73
Sukkah
2b 73
20a 11, 23
28a 16, 30, 151
35b 30
44a 11
45b 8, 21
Beitzah
5a 103, 120
5b 103
11b 115
Rosh Hashanah
7b 146
28b 100
29b 102, 110
31b 64
Ta'anit
2a 98
17b 30
Megillah
2b 94, 108
3a 94, 152

19b 7, 9, 20, 86
25a 120, 130
32a 60, 150
Mo'ed Katan
17a 51
19a 116, 129
Chagigah
4a 30
14a 138
15b 151
18a 28, 41
Yevamot
14a 17
21a 30, 99
42b 148
49b 149
62a 67
72b 141
79a 60
86b 60
88a 102
90b 95, 97, 102, 108
111b 142
Ketubot
20a 29
22a 83, 89
28a 35
39a 149
40b 55
46b 67
49b 64
51a 67
65b 67
71a 142
95b 67
104a 121, 131
Nedarim 28b 64
Nazir 47b 36
Sotah
14a 85, 90

47b 11, 16
48a 60
49b 61

Gittin
12a 55
17a 65
29a 146, 157
36a 102, 109, 117, 129
36b 102, 109
45b 69
59a–b 68
60b 149
64a 29
65a 35

Kiddushin
3b 36
4b 36
29a 67
31a 73
32a 127
49b 116
57b 30
66b 130
68b 121, 130
69a 54
81b 57

Bava Kama
46b 35
79b 104, 110
82a 31, 44, 60, 67
87a 73
102a 147, 148, 157

Bava Metzia
30b 127
33a 150
59b 94, 107, 144, 156, 176
83a 126, 132
90a 124, 131
100a 29
114a 149

116a 149
Bava Batra
5b 29
12a 2, 18
21a 64
33a 29
59b 160
60b 64, 104, 111
65b 142
Sanhedrin
4b 31
25b 68
27b 29
68b 52
71a 52, 53
74a 49, 58
78a 30, 43
86a 137, 142, 155
88b 11, 12, 16, 23, 100
89b 103
99a 84, 89
Shevuot
23b 35
25b 51
48b 149
Makkot 23 36
Avodah Zarah
6b 51
7a 148
35a 143
36a 103, 105, 111
36b 60
Horiyot 13b 143
Zevachim
49b 36
119b 96
Menachot 67a 123, 131
Chullin
5b 64

27a 31
84a 146
95b 149
Bekhorot 8a 40
Temurah
13b 51
14b 95
16a 10, 22, 94, 107
28b 96
Niddah
11b 148
19b 84
30b 40
32a 30
Talmud (Jerusalem)
Pe'ah 2:4 7, 20
Shevi'it 4:2 104
Challah 3:1 124, 131
Shabbat 1:4 105
Yevamot
1:6 144
4:12 116
Ketubot
1:1 60
11:3 67
Gittin 4:3 65
Avodah Zarah 2:7 10, 22
Taryag p. 28 75
Tashbatz
1:1:151 37
2:9 2
Taz, *Yoreh De'ah* 293:4 16
Three Great Systems of Jurisprudence, p. 160 118
Tiferet Yisrael, Eduyot 1:5 103
Tosafot
Shabbat
81b 149
135a 30
Pesachim 50a 103, 110

Sukkah
5a 40
28a 151
Beitzah 5a 121
Yevamot
7b 34
42b 149
88a 102
90b 97, 108
Gittin 36a 117
Bava Metzia 59b 94
Sanhedrin 89b 97
Avodah Zarah
35a 103, 110
57b 103, 110
Menachot 92b 32
Tosafot Rid, Shabbat 31a 55
Tosefot Yeshanim, Yevamot 90b 97
Tosefot Yom-Tov
Sotah 9:1 149, 158
Eduyot 1:5 103
Zevachim 10:2 34
Introduction to *Berachot* 10, 22
Tosefta
Shevi'it 3 104
Pesachim 2:6 119, 130
Eduyot 1:1 137, 145, 155
Tradition, Vol. 9, nos. 1 and 2 7
Tur, Choshen Mishpat 97
Turei Even, Chagigah 6a 73
Rav Osher Weiss, *Parashat Mishpatim* 5778 *Kovetz* 1854
Rav Yonatan Eibeshutz
Kreti, Yoreh De'ah, Trefut 29 (1:5) 28, 41
Urim vTumim 2, 18
Yam Shel Shlomo, Introduction to *Chullin* 152
Yesod HaMishnah V'Arichatah 17, 147
Yismach Moshe, p. 20 126

The fonts used in this book are from the Arno family

Maggid Books
The best of contemporary Jewish thought from
Koren Publishers Jerusalem Ltd.